Windswept Ridgeway near Kingston Russell.

FOLLOWING PAGES
Two of the Ridgeway's most well known landmarks,
the Hell Stone, a Neolithic chambered long barrow, and Hardy Monument on Black Down.

THE DOVECOTE PRESS

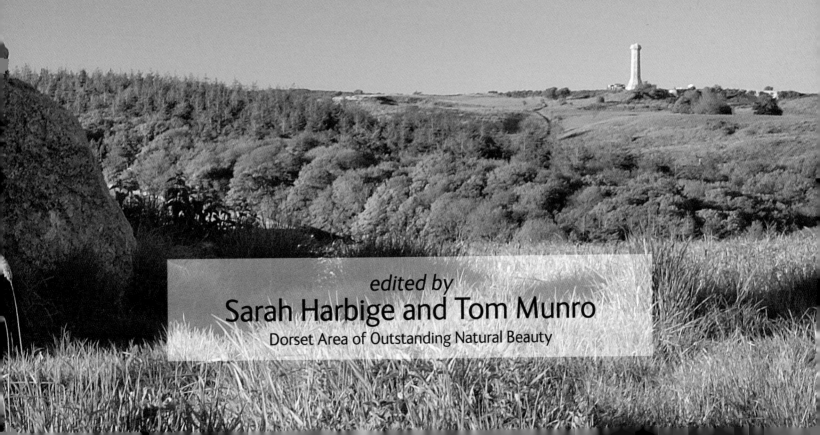

SOUTH DORSET RIDGEWAY

edited by
Sarah Harbige and Tom Munro
Dorset Area of Outstanding Natural Beauty

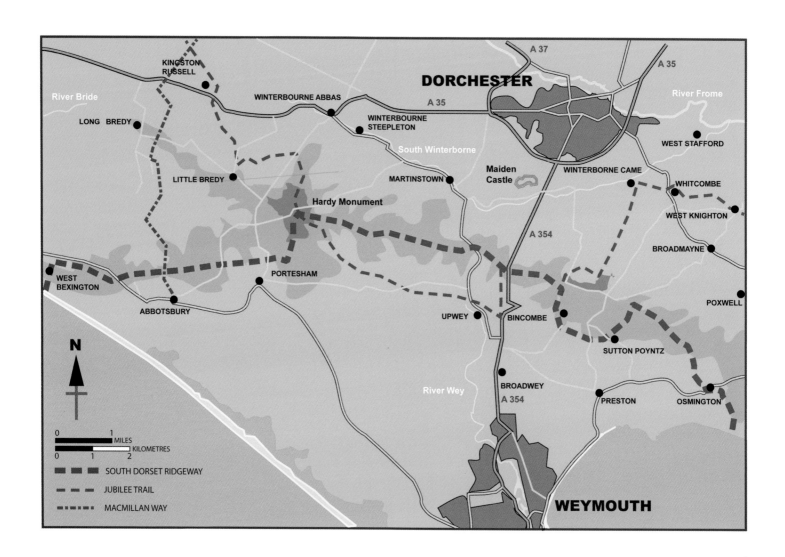

CONTENTS

Galloping the Ridgeway. The ridge is crossed by a network of bridleways which make it a popular horse riding area. St Catherine's Chapel, Abbotsbury, is in the background.

INTRODUCTION

'The English landscape itself, to those who know how to read it right, is the richest historical record we possess ... there are discoveries to be made in it for which no written documents exist, or have ever existed.'

W.G. Hoskins in Christopher Taylor,
The Making of the English Landscape: Dorset (2004)

THE SOUTH DORSET RIDGEWAY is a chalk ridge lying from east to west across the south of the county and is one of the most distinctive pieces of landscape in the country. The area is bordered by the English Channel coast to the south and the Frome river valley in the north; from the villages of Abbotsbury and Long Bredy in the west to Poxwell in the east. This relatively small area, at most only 25 km long and 10 km wide, provides an introduction to the best that the British countryside has to offer. It is home to a remarkable ancient ceremonial landscape, mixed with some of the most spectacular coastal and inland scenery in the UK. The area is well known by local residents but less so by those from further afield. This guide will share some of the secrets of the ridge and tell some of its stories. The South Dorset Ridgeway deserves to be explored further and for its historical record to become more widely understood.

The Ridgeway's international significance is based upon one of the most diverse Neolithic and Bronze Age landscapes in Europe. It has been suggested that nowhere else in the country has such

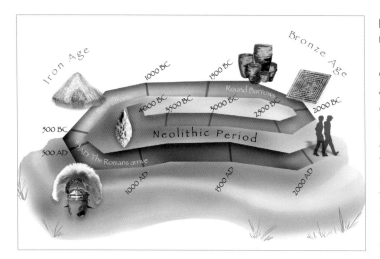

Ridgeway Timeline, showing the historical periods relevant to the long history of the South Dorset Ridgeway. Illustration by Yvonne Lee.

plough changed the look of the land and in lower-lying areas eroded much of the historical evidence left by earlier communities.

Long after the monuments' prehistoric architects had passed on, the impact of the Ridgeway landscape was felt by later writers and travellers, particularly through the seventeenth and eighteenth centuries. The area was commented on by travellers such as Celia Fiennes (1697/8) and Daniel Defoe (1724) and antiquarians John Aubrey (1687) and William Stukely (1723). However it was thanks to the work of the Dorset rector John Hutchins (1698-1773), who recorded the *History and Antiquities of Dorset* that we have the first systematic record of the historical landscape. Later antiquarians Charles Warne (1866) and L.V. Grinsell (1959) tried to make some sense of hundreds of round barrows. Dorset is also fortunate to be the subject of a full survey of its historic monuments by the Royal Commission on Historical Monuments, published from the 1950s to the 1970s. More recent studies and research include work by Peter Woodward (1983) and ongoing studies begun as part of the South Dorset Ridgeway Heritage Project (2008-2011). Recent archaeological and historical research has discovered new stories to tell, and hopefully will continue do so in the future.

The South Dorset Ridgeway has been known by several names, including The Dorset Coastal Ridgeway, The Great Southern Ridgeway and just The Coastal Ridgeway. The names given to such routes come into being long after their first use as a way of moving people and animals across the landscape. It is a received wisdom that since ancient times open uplands must have been a route as they helped people move about quickly and freely, keeping clear of wooded and muddy valley bottoms. Whether they were used as long distance links, joining up with other routes across Wessex can only be guessed at. However as one recent commentator, David Viner, has said, the South Dorset Ridgeway can hardly be bettered as an experience in

dramatic use been made of the topography and underlying geology for the construction of historic monuments. These landscapes were purposefully designed to have a strong visual impact and to convey a message to both locals and incomers to the area. The monuments were placed specifically to be seen from the settlements and from each other. They include Neolithic causewayed enclosures and unique bank barrows, immense henge monuments and more intimate stone circles, an incredibly dense group of almost 1000 Bronze Age round barrows, as well as later Iron Age hillforts.

The fact that these archaeological sites have survived is fortunate. Many are located on high ground that has not been transformed by later generations. There is no doubt that agriculture has had the biggest impact on this landscape – woodland clearance and the tracing high level, long distance prehistoric routes.

As farming evolved through the Neolithic and more land was taken into cultivation other tracks would have opened up to link communities to their fields, their ceremonial sites and to each other. Trade stimulated movement across large areas – Neolithic farmers traded stone axes right across the country. Archaeological finds such as the shard of a Cornish Neolithic pot found in Sutton Poyntz demonstrate a trading network on a scale that needed good communication links and well-defined routes. It is not hard to imagine groups of people moving across the Ridgeway to gather at the causewayed enclosure at Maiden Castle or the henge monuments in what is now Dorchester.

Many of the ancient Ridgeways now form the backbone of the long distance National Trail network. The South Dorset Ridgeway is no exception and has been part of the South West Coast Path since its completion in 1978. The current footpath follows the line of the ridge for most of its route, but it's easy to recognise where the path leaves the original trackway.

The character of the Ridgeway landscape is very much determined by its underlying geology as you move from west to east. The high chalk downland is at its widest at its western end, at around 10 km. It is characterised by rounded hills and small patches of woodland, often home to coveys of partridge and pheasant. The valley of the River Bride divides the area into two spurs of high ground. The ancient trackways use these spurs to travel north and on to the west. The northern branch crosses the hills from the present A35 and the route west clings to the steep escarpment above the coast. The routes were recognised in the 1024 Saxon Charter of Portesham, in which the path west of Gould's Hill to Martin's Down was known as 'eald wag' (Old Way), and the path south to Abbotsbury hillfort across White Hill was called 'straet'.

The South Dorset Ridgeway is at its most striking in its central

Early summer below the Hardy Monument.

section, with a steep escarpment to the south and gentler northern slopes towards the South Winterborne valley and Dorchester. The area is characterised by chalk streams flowing west to east and dry combes or valleys that run up to the narrow heath-covered ridge. The underlying chalk here is capped by a layer of gravels and sands which brings about a change in ground cover from the grass-covered downland elsewhere along the Ridgeway. Heathland plants such as heather and bilberry abound. The skyline here is dominated by the nineteenth century Hardy Monument, proudly standing above the ridge and visible from miles around.

The Ridgeway area narrows as it nears the sea in the east. The coastline of Weymouth Bay lies to the south and to the north the wide valley of the River Frome leads the eye towards the subdued colours of the Dorset heaths. The parishes to the north of the ridge are marked by long strips of land within their boundaries that include pasture up to the Ridgeway. The villages below the steep escarpment to the south have grown up around the spring line and sources of water that now go on to meet the demands of the holiday resort of Weymouth. From Weymouth the Ridgeway is distinguished by two distinct landmarks. A Bronze Age barrow group, known locally as Bincombe Bumps, is visible from most of the town. Further to the east is the Osmington White Horse, the only chalk hill figure of a horse and rider in the country; it has sat above the town on its never-ending journey east since 1808.

Today the focus of the Ridgeway continues to be agriculture. It is also a centre for leisure activity, used by walkers along the South West Coast Path National Trail and by cyclists and horse riders on the many paths and bridleways.

Now part of the National Trail Network, the South Dorset Ridgeway follows the line of older routes.

The South Dorset Ridgeway from the Purbeck Ridge above Poxwell. The Osmington White Horse is visible in the middle of the photograph.

GEOLOGY

Sam Scriven

'A more varied or more beautiful country is nowhere to be seen in England than from Dorchester all the way to Bridport, and well worth a long journey to see.'
Arthur Young,
A Farmer's Tour through the East of England (1771)

Underlying a landscape, and often taken for granted is the bedrock. In Dorset the geology of the coast has been given World Heritage Status but away from the coast, inland, the rocks beneath our feet create the rolling hills, green vales and dramatic high ridges. Upon this landscape humans have made their mark and few places can tell that story better than the South Dorset Ridgeway.

On a clear day from Rocket Quarry near Portesham one can see east along the ridge to Bincombe, south to Portland and west to Abbotsbury. From here the countryside between the South Dorset Ridgeway and Weymouth appears as a series of ridges and vales running east-west. This entire landscape has formed because the rocks here have been folded up into something known to geologists as an anticline – a dome shaped fold.

Around 40 million years ago Africa collided with Europe to form the Alps. The tremendous forces that crumpled and buckled rocks in southern Europe to create mountains were felt as far north as southern Britain, creating large, but relatively gentle folds in our geology. Around Weymouth the layers of rock were folded upwards into a linear 'anticline'. The middle or 'axis' of this fold runs east to west on a line that can be traced roughly through Lodmoor Country Park and Bagwell Farm. The easiest place to see the way the rocks have been tilted is by looking at Portland. Portland slopes down to the sea at Portland Bill in a southerly direction.

To make things more complicated the Weymouth anticline was imprinted over a much older feature of the geology, where all the layers of rock also dip gently towards the east. This has created a fold that 'closes' if you follow it eastward. What that means is that the layers of rock that are repeated in the northern and southern limbs appear to 'join up' across the fold axis working east.

During and after the formation of the Weymouth anticline, erosion has cut down into the uplifted geology. This has created the landscape between the Ridgeway and Portland. The hard bands such as the Chalk, Corallian limestone and Forest Marble have left ridges while the soft rocks like the Kimmeridge and Oxford Clays have been eroded into vales. These features have an east-west orientation reflecting the orientation of the anticline.

The highest ridge in this geologically-controlled landscape is made of chalk and the very shape of it is dictated by the anticline. The northern side of the ridge slopes gently away because it follows the dipping surface of the layers within the bedrock. This is known as the dip-slope. On the southern side erosion has cut down through these layers making a much steeper slope known as the scarp. 'Scarp and dip' is a classic geological landscape feature.

At Rocket Quarry local people used to extract Portland and Purbeck Limestone for building. To find the part of the southern limb of the fold to match the geology of Rocket Quarry we have to look to the

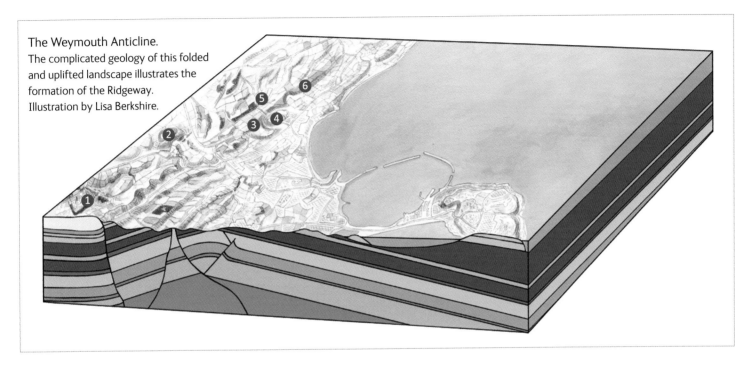

The Weymouth Anticline.
The complicated geology of this folded and uplifted landscape illustrates the formation of the Ridgeway.
Illustration by Lisa Berkshire.

Isle of Portland where Portland and Purbeck limestone is still quarried. Looking eleven miles across to Portland from Rocket Quarry gives a good indication of the scale of the Weymouth anticline and of the amount of erosion that has taken place to create the landscape we see today.

Although this larger landscape is the result of a single geological feature there is only one contender for the rock that characterises the South Dorset Ridgeway – chalk. Chalk is a pure limestone that formed at the end of the cretaceous period between about 65 and 95 million years ago. At that time much of England would have

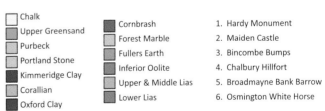

☐ Chalk
◻ Upper Greensand
◻ Purbeck
◻ Portland Stone
■ Kimmeridge Clay
◻ Corallian
■ Oxford Clay

◼ Cornbrash
◻ Forest Marble
◻ Fullers Earth
◻ Inferior Oolite
◻ Upper & Middle Lias
◻ Lower Lias

1. Hardy Monument
2. Maiden Castle
3. Bincombe Bumps
4. Chalbury Hillfort
5. Broadmayne Bank Barrow
6. Osmington White Horse

been submerged in a warm tropical sea teeming with life. Over time trillions of microscopic skeletons left behind by plankton accumulated on the seabed. With no other sediment being deposited,

The view from the Hardy Monument across the Weymouth anticline to Portland. The bell heather in the foreground is a common plant found on the heaths of Dorset. The area of the Ridgeway around the Hardy Monument is a rare pocket of heath along a chalk ridge.

A large tufa 'log' that formed around a fossilised tree 140 million years ago.

Rocket Quarry, 1896, showing the tufa 'log'.

Coccoliths, calcium carbonate remains of tiny sea creatures, magnified under an electron scanning microscope.

the calcium carbonate remains of these tiny sea creatures built up, forming extraordinarily thick layers. Other creatures such as sponges contributed silica into this sediment and this, through a complicated and still not well understood geological process, formed the nodules of flint synonymous with chalk. These nodules often formed inside the branching burrows of creatures living on the chalk seabed giving them their odd shapes.

It is easy to see why, for thousands of years, the chalk ridges of England have attracted settlements. They were a source of flint, the material vital for making the earliest tools, freshwater springs are often found associated with chalk and the well-draining high ground was perfect for easy travel and for positioning monuments like barrows. Any explanation of the long human history of the Ridgeway and the reasons man first made it his home must always begin with the geology.

ARCHAEOLOGY

The Grey Mare and her Colts by local artist Peter Emery.

NEOLITHIC RIDGEWAY

Hazel Riley

The landscape of the South Dorset Ridgeway contains some of the most remarkable evidence for the way that our distant ancestors lived in the period that archaeologists call the Neolithic: the years between 4000 and 2000 BC. During this period the Ridgeway landscape was transformed. Originally a tangled mass of woodland threaded with the paths that Mesolithic hunters took on their quest for deer with the odd small clearing, it became an open landscape with extensive cleared areas between Long Bredy and Winterbourne Steepleton, around Maiden Castle and Dorchester, and up on Came Down. These people were some of the first farmers in England and, like farmers today, they

'. . . it is certain that every enquiring spectator must be equally struck with this extraordinary district . . . where the adjacent downs or the lofty Ridgeway with its prolonged upland crest are gracefully undulated with these time-honoured memorials.'
Charles Warne
Celtic Tumuli of Dorset (1866)

The South Dorset Ridgeway offers an insight into how landscape is shaped by the people who have lived there. The earliest human remains and artefacts date from 100,000 BC and were discovered towards the eastern end of the ridge at Bincombe. The earliest monuments from about 4000 to 2000 BC occur along its entire length. Large earthen mounds and enclosures survive, as do stone monuments. These are focussed at the western end, within reach of the easy supply of material from one of the Ridgeway's most extraordinary sites – the Valley of the Stones.

Between 2500 and 2000 BC during the Late Neolithic and Early Bronze Age the building of monuments continued on either side of the South Winterborne Valley. To the south and along the high ground dramatic funerary mounds were constructed, strung out along the ridge top like pearls. To the north towards the River Frome substantial circular timber henge monuments were built. These would become focal points for the surrounding groups of people well into the next millennium. In the Iron Age (600 BC to AD 43) the focus of activity stayed in this lower lying landscape, with the adaptation of Maiden Castle into an enormous hillfort.

Neolithic flint arrowheads found during excavations at Thomas Hardye School, Dorchester.

Roe deer remain common on the Ridgeway today, and their ancestors provided food for Neolithic hunters.

Maiden Castle during the Neolithic, 4000 – 2000 BC. The bank barrow and causewayed enclosure are clearly visible on the top of the hill.
Illustration by Peter Dunn.

worked with the Ridgeway landscape and knew it intimately. They lived just off the ridge tops in places like Rowden and Sutton Poyntz, where they grew barley and wheat; kept pigs, sheep and cattle.

The Neolithic farmers made their mark on the Ridgeway in two ways: by clearing woodland and marking out enclosures and fields, and by building monuments to celebrate both life and death. The bones of the dead were buried in chambers, kept safe under long, earthen mounds and used for successive burials over a few hundred

Mount Pleasant Henge was built in about 2500 BC and is about 370 metres in diameter. It had four causewayed entrances and an internal timber palisade about 245 metres by 270 metres with only two small entrances. It was occupied at various times until the Iron Age. Archaeologists have also found Roman and Saxon remains on the site. Now only visible from the air, the henge monument has been destroyed by ploughing, probably from as early on as the Iron Age.

Excavations in 1984-6 in the former Greyhound Yard in Dorchester discovered a host of finds, including 21 massive post pits, believed to be the remains of one side of a huge henge monument. It has been estimated that the henge could have been as much as 380 metres in diameter, and it was built between 2900 to 2340 BC. The site has since been built upon but an indication of its size can be seen in the car park below Waitrose. Illustration by John Hodgson.

years before being finally blocked and sealed. Wander up to the Grey Mare and her Colts as the mist lifts on a spring morning and you can see why the Ridgeway was chosen as a special place 4000 years ago.

On the hill now occupied by the massive Iron Age earthworks of Maiden Castle are traces of a much older earthwork: a causewayed enclosure, an important place on the Ridgeway around 3500 BC, where people who were scattered rather sparsely across the landscape could come together to feast, trade and, sometimes, leave dead bodies to endure the gruesome (to our eyes) process of

excarnation, the exposure of dead bodies before burial. The enclosure was effectively sealed by the construction of a long earthen mound over it, one of three massive bank barrows on the Ridgeway. Those at Long Bredy and Broadmayne were carefully situated at prominent positions at the east and west ends of the Ridgeway and they remain iconic features in the landscape today.

The area around Dorchester continued to be a focus for human settlements as the linear forms of the long barrows and bank barrows were replaced by impressive circular henge monuments which, like causewayed enclosures, seemed to have marked important spaces, perhaps including or excluding certain groups of people. The earthworks of Maumbury Rings, originally built as a Neolithic henge monument then converted into an amphitheatre by the Romans, can still be seen right in the centre of Dorchester, but other sites, like the massive enclosure at Mount Pleasant, have been ploughed for many hundreds of years and are now only visible from the air, while the much smaller pit circles at the foot of Conygar Hill were only discovered when topsoil was stripped during the construction of the Dorchester by-pass, hinting that there is still more to discover about the first farmers of the Ridgeway.

THE BRONZE AGE
John Gale

The Bronze Age is weakly defined, but relates to an approximate 1,200 year period during which people used similar materials and built similar structures. The boundaries between the end of the Neolithic and the beginning of the Bronze Age, and likewise the boundary marking the transition to the Iron Age are broad. This overlap applies to monuments as well as individual finds and is a reminder of the continual evolution of the daily way of life of our early ancestors.

The Bronze Age is a label referring to the technological leap in metalworking which occurred around 3000 BC; this technology's time period is shared with related styles of features and artefacts, some of which occur in great quantities on the South Dorset Ridgeway.

Undoubtedly the monument which dominates the surviving Bronze Age landscape of the Ridgeway is that of the round barrow. They litter the undulating hillsides and hilltops and are frequent reminders of the presence of our ancestors within this ancient landscape. These round

Jane Brayne's illustration of a Bronze Age funeral at Bincombe Down. 'Dancers circle a collared urn containing the burnt remains of one of their community.'

mounds had a funeral purpose; many that have been dug over the centuries have produced human remains – both inhumations and cremations. These burials were sometime accompanied by grave goods.

The most celebrated example of the round barrow is found to the north-east of Martinstown on Clandon Hill. An incomplete excavation by Edward Cunnington in 1883 revealed a collection of fine artefacts including a gold lozenge (probably worn on the chest) very similar to the more famous example excavated at Bush barrow near Stonehenge. The finds from Cunnington's excavation are on display at the Dorset County Museum and provide a rare glimpse into the technological and artistic accomplishments of people who lived on the Ridgeway around 2000 BC. However, excavation has revealed

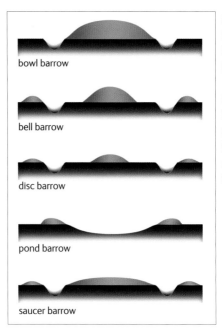

Left Shapes of round barrows found on the South Dorset Ridgeway. Illustration by Yvonne Lee.

Right The Clandon Lozenge. Perhaps one of the most spectacular archaeological finds along the Ridgeway and now on display in Dorset County Museum.

that such monuments are unlikely to be solely for burials and may have functioned as important ceremonial and cultural places that were in use for extended periods of time.

Alongside the round barrows, the Ridgeway has a number of other Bronze Age monuments that are also considered to be linked to the ceremonial and ritual activities of the time. The stone circles at Winterbourne Abbas, Hampton and Kingston Russell are all examples of ceremonial centres that are likely to have been in use at the time the barrows were being built; similarly the Late Neolithic henge monuments at Maumbury Rings and Mount Pleasant (both in Dorchester) continued in use at this time.

Similarities with Stonehenge or perhaps more correctly with the Stonehenge landscape do not end there. The quantity and range of monument types of both the South Dorset Ridgeway and Stonehenge are very comparable and strongly indicate a shared heritage and purpose. The similarities are so strong that it's tempting to suggest that both areas functioned as 'central cultural cores' where the rituals and ceremonies of the community were carried out for successive generations.

Unfortunately our knowledge of where these people were living on or around the Ridgeway is less well understood but as farmers they probably lived in small communities within the fields they farmed. A tantalising glimpse of one such settlement was excavated at Rowden near Winterbourne Steepleton and was dated to the later Bronze Age. Here, like Bronze Age sites elsewhere on the downs of southern England, were the remains of a small round hut of lightly built timbers. This would have sheltered a small family who farmed the land immediately around them creating a small farmstead.

THE IRON AGE
Martin Papworth

The Iron Age is the latest period before the first written sources provide history. It begins in obscurity, soon after 800 BC, when the first iron object was brought into Britain and the art of iron production was shared with the local people. It ends with the Roman Conquest of AD 43-44, when the first named people (the *Durotriges*), place (*Dunium*) and person (the invading Roman commander Vespasian who later became Emperor of Rome) can be tentatively linked to Dorset. The Ridgeway people would have undergone great social changes between the beginning and end of the Iron Age.

During this period, the Ridgeway continued to be used as an important routeway. The people living in the area seem to have respected the Bronze Age burial mounds but did not bury their dead there. Evidence suggests they had a different belief system, closely linked to agricultural production. Bodies and parts of bodies are found in old grain storage pits, mixed with animal bones and other items – as though the dead were thrown away like rubbish. However, the deposits found in the backfilled pits probably represent complex rituals that are difficult to understand without written records.

The typical monument of the Iron Age is the hillfort. Now they can be seen as rings of grass covered ramparts and ditches. When they were first built these earthworks were deeper and steeper, bright white from freshly dug chalk topped with timber palisades with great timber gates guarding the entrances. Dorset boasts the best hillforts in Britain and Maiden Castle is the most famous and awe-inspiring of them all.

Several other hillforts relate to the South Dorset Ridgeway. To the west above Abbotsbury village is Abbotsbury Castle; to the south-

Maiden Castle at the height of its Iron Age occupation in about 200 BC. Compare this illustration with the view of development during the Neolithic on page 17. The surrounding area shows evidence of farming and settlement. Illustration by Peter Dunn.

east is Chalbury Hill and beside Dorchester and the River Frome is Poundbury Camp. The ramparts of each enclose about 6 hectares, and in 600 BC, when first constructed, Maiden Castle was also this size. By 450 BC, it had been enlarged to 19 hectares and was packed with round houses and grain storage pits. At this time, Chalbury was abandoned with Poundbury and Abbotsbury containing less than 10 houses each. Maiden Castle grew to become the principal and virtually

The Whitcombe Warrior. The burial of a young Iron Age man at Whitcombe near Broadmayne. He was probably buried fully clothed and may have been still wearing his sword. There was also a small axe head, spindle whorl and brooch. The man's possessions and the care given to his burial suggest he was important within his social group. He was called the Whitcombe Warrior because of his sword, but there is no evidence of him having fought in a battle. He can be seen in Dorset County Museum.

now seen as earthworks along the Ridgeway in places like the Valley of the Stones near Long Bredy.

Cemeteries are often found outside the farm enclosures, evidence of a new distinctive south Dorset burial rite. Instead of body parts placed in storage pits, the dead were buried in shallow oval graves. They were laid to rest in a crouched position accompanied by joints of meat and groups of pots, presumably food and drink for the after-life. In the richer graves other personal objects are found, such as the sword found with the so-called Whitcombe Warrior, the decorated bronze mirror found with a woman at Portesham and the group of gaming counters placed beside a young man at Puncknowle.

In the last 100 years before the Roman Conquest, increasing trade contact with the expanding Roman world introduced new ideas and products to the people of the Ridgeway. They started to use coins. As the designs on these are unique to the Dorset area, they have been seen as a tribal emblem of a people known as the *Durotriges*. This name is first recorded by a Greek geographer called Ptolemy in the second century AD.

It is believed that the people of Maiden Castle and the surrounding farmsteads were hostile to Rome and fought the invaders. Mortimer Wheeler, who excavated Maiden Castle in the 1930s, interpreted the skeletons he found with sword cuts to the bones as evidence of a battle at the hillfort. More recently, archaeologists have suggested that the battle between the Romans and British took place some distance from the site.

Once occupied and absorbed into the Roman Empire, the local people adopted Roman ways and their homes gradually changed from round houses to villas. Their beliefs may have altered more slowly. For example, for many decades the Ridgeway people did not cremate their dead in the Roman fashion but continued their distinctive burial rite.

the only settlement in the area. This dominance lasted until about 100 BC when the local political system changed, Maiden Castle's population began to decline and new farmsteads were created in the surrounding landscape, particularly along the Frome valley.

These farms, like the one excavated near Maiden Castle Road, typically consisted of a bank and ditch with a single gate enclosing two or three round houses, a few storage pits and groups of four post-holes, interpreted as the remains of granaries. From here, families would have cultivated the field systems in use since the Bronze Age. These farmed areas consisted of clusters of small rectangular fields,

ROMAN RIDGEWAY

The invading Roman Legion II Augusta worked west through southern Britain under the command of Vespasian. It is clear they met some opposition from locals, particularly at Hod Hill near Blandford. The Roman writer Suetonius later recorded that Vespasian *'went to Britain, where he fought thirty battles, conquered two war-like tribes and captures more than twenty towns, besides the whole of the Isle of Wight.'* It is unlikely Vespasian conquered the Durotriges but the towns may well refer to the hillforts of Dorset.

Local residents took on board the Roman lifestyle, settling in the newly created urban centre of Durnovaria (Dorchester). The Legion's impact on the Ridgeway is concentrated on the road network that crossed or made use of existing high ground and a possible signal station at Black Down.

Roads were built primarily by the army to move its men and supplies around the country. They were built in straight lines with little regard to what went before, whether it was a farm or a hill. Dorchester became a hub for these roads at the Frome river crossing. The road south to the Roman port crossed the Ridgeway close to the line of the present A354 to Weymouth. There may well have been other smaller road crossings too. A small enclosure at Black Down (SY603880) has been recorded as a Roman signal station, linking Dorchester with the Roman Fort at Waddon Hill (ST445015) near Stoke Abbott in west Dorset. However more recent interpretation suggests the Black Down enclosure could be much older.

By far the biggest impact on the landscape of the Ridgeway has been agriculture. It has dominated land use for at least 6000 years and we can assume that during the Roman period (AD 43-410) this did

Maiden Castle's ceremonial or ritual significance continued over a long time. The hillfort had probably contained a temple or religious site during the Iron Age and in the mid fourth century there was a revival in paganism in Britain. At this time a small temple was constructed to the Goddess Minerva, perhaps on the site of an earlier shrine. Meaningfully, the building which contained a central block surrounded by a corridor or portico could be seen from the town.

not change. The evidence of surviving 'Celtic' field systems indicates widespread cultivation of grain crops from at least the Bronze Age, if not earlier. These fields would have been in continual use by descendents of these original farmers. Demand for local markets and export would have been significant. Estimates of population growth suggest that during the Romano-British period five million people lived in Britain, five times more than during the Iron Age. Projects such as the National Mapping Programme have found potential Romano-British enclosures, farmsteads and settlements in the valleys surrounding the Ridgeway.

The formal changes in lifestyle and administration influenced by

Members of the Roman re-enactment group, Legio II Augusta, at an event in Dorchester.

Roman rule was centred on urban areas and steadily filtered through to the countryside. A Romano-British farmer would very much have lived as his ancestors had, gradually adopting new crops and livestock such as rye, oats, plums and chickens. He may also have rebuilt his house in the Roman style, a rectangular stone building with a tiled roof and plastered walls. Farming was hard work but imported technology included an iron tip for the plough or 'ard', which made ploughing a little easier and meant heavier, clay soils could be put under cultivation. Although the remains of some Romano-British farms and settlements survive on high ground in Dorset those of the South Dorset Ridgeway appear to have been obscured by later land use.

THE PIT OF DOOM
Steve Wallis

The Weymouth Relief Road (A354) is a section of new road between the Ridgeway and Weymouth that was constructed between 2008 and 2011. It is the latest means of transporting people and goods across the Ridgeway – a Roman road crosses the Ridgeway just to the west, Isambard Kingdom Brunel's railway of the 1850s runs through Bincombe tunnel beneath the road, and much of the new road replaced a turnpike road constructed in 1823.

Today, the proper care of our archaeological heritage is an important part of major developments such as this road's construction. As part of the planning of the scheme, lots of research and archaeological

An osteologist (bone specialist) from Oxford Archaeology carefully cleaning and recording a burial in the pit.

fieldwork was carried out to find out what effect the construction work would have on archaeological remains and what could be done about it. The route across the Ridgeway was designed to avoid two surviving barrows. These barrows are no longer ploughed and can be seen on either side of the new road.

One of the first phases of construction was a major archaeological excavation on the top of the South Dorset Ridgeway in late 2008. This dig was effectively the biggest sample of the Ridgeway that has ever been excavated and as well as the barrows gives us a good idea of the range of other archaeological features that are present. Oxford Archaeology found chalk quarries, boundaries and farm tracks of various dates, and in particular there were fifteen human burials dating from the Neolithic and the Bronze Age. Some were simply placed in holes in the ground, while others were in cists, which are settings of upright stones that surrounded the body. They are particularly important in showing that the Ridgeway as a whole was used for burial, not just the barrows. A Bronze Age barrow whose mound had been destroyed by ploughing was also excavated; several burials from the Roman period had been dug into it. Another unexpected find was a workshop or store used by the men who built the railway during the 1850s.

In May 2009, a surprise discovery was made during the removal of a hedge at the edge of the area excavated the previous year: human skeletons were found. Detailed archaeological recording over the next couple of months found this to be a disused quarry pit into which had been thrown the bodies of over fifty adult males, all of whom had been decapitated with the heads piled in one corner of the pit.

When all the bodies were exposed, the sight was both visually stunning and grisly, and the nickname 'The Pit of Doom' given to it by the construction team seems to have stuck. The discovery attracted national and international interest. At the time of writing,

The 'Pit of Doom'. Look closely to see how the torsos had been flung into the pit in a haphazard fashion.

we know that the mass burial dates between AD 910 and 1030, and those buried there came from various locations but mostly from what is now Sweden – some from north of the Arctic Circle. The majority were young men who had been in good health. These factors all suggest the execution of a party of Vikings. It is a matter of continuing debate as to whether they were raiders, settlers or part of an army, and whether they were killed by the local Saxon militia or their compatriots. But hopefully more will be revealed as further analysis of their remains continues.

Celtic fields at Crow Hill near Littlebredy and the Valley of the Stones. A Bronze Age round house is visible as a circular feature in the foreground.

THE RIDGEWAY FROM THE AIR
Andrew Young

The view of the South Dorset Ridgeway from the air shows the astonishing richness of its archaeological remains. Bronze Age barrows, ancient fields and magnificent Iron Age hillforts are all laid out before you and their patterns can be appreciated in a unique way. Since the earliest days of aviation archaeologists have realised the importance of aerial photography as a tool for understanding archaeological sites and for discovering new ones. Recent work on the Ridgeway includes a survey of its archaeology using aerial photographs.

There are two types of aerial photograph. The first are specialist photos specifically targeting archaeological sites, taken from low-flying aircraft at an oblique or slanting angle, so that light and shadow show the site at its best. The second are vertical photographs taken for non-archaeological reasons and covering large areas of the landscape. The most important verticals were taken by the RAF just after the Second World War and show the countryside as it was before the onset of intensive agriculture. During the National Mapping programme study 11,000 photographs were examined and all visible sites were systematically drawn and recorded, from the Neolithic monuments right up to the pillboxes and other abandoned defences from the Second World War.

Dorset is fortunate in that many of its ancient monuments survive as upstanding monuments. However, some have been levelled by ploughing. These can still be seen on aerial photographs as tell-tale marks in freshly ploughed fields or in fields of ripening crops. For instance Bronze Age barrows usually consist of a central mound surrounded by an outer ditch cut into the chalk. Over time the ditch would become filled with topsoil material which will then show as a dark stain in a ploughed field.

Bronze Age enclosure at Tenant's Hill. The D-shaped enclosure is contemporary with the field banks to its right.

As long ago as 1500 BC much of the land around the Ridgeway was being farmed. There is evidence of widespread arable cultivation in the form of 'Celtic' fields. Over time ploughed soil gradually worked its way down slope to form lynchets – substantial build-ups of soil piled against the banks. In places the small houses of these Bronze Age farmers can be seen set in the corners of the fields. Many of the Celtic fields are overlain by ridge and furrow – the parallel plough marks made by medieval farmers.

Other Bronze Age settlements were housed in enclosures and enclosed settlements are also characteristic of the Iron Age. In the Roman period a new form of settlement, or village, appeared on the Ridgeway. These villages consist of small rectangular enclosures or 'tofts' – small plots containing houses – arranged on one or both sides of a single street.

This National Mapping Programme has illustrated the extraordinary wealth of archaeology of the Ridgeway by recording more than 3,000 sites. The importance of the survey is underlined by the fact that two thirds of these were previously unrecorded and were newly identified during the project. The new sites were found in all parts of the Ridgeway and include many barrows, two small Neolithic henge monuments, Iron Age enclosures and a possible Romano-British village at Little Hogleaze.

RIDGEWAY COMMUNITIES

There have been communities of people living and working around the South Dorset Ridgeway for millennia and evidence of their settlement can still be seen today. Mesolithic people (8000-3500 BC) hunted and fished in the valleys and the lower lying areas towards the coast. They were succeeded by Neolithic farmers (4000-2000 BC), whose way of life depended on mixed farming with crops and animal husbandry. People worked together to clear land of trees to create open farmland with huge communal monuments and burial places. From 2000 BC, while cultural practices changed with the emergence of the

Bronze Age, the pattern of land clearance continued. The number of monuments created around modern Dorchester at this time suggests a good size population in the Frome and South Winterborne valleys. In the succeeding years the population continued to grow, there was more pressure on the land and a number of settlements were created on higher ground.

During the next cultural shift, the Iron Age (which begins around 600 BC), there is evidence of a scale of civil organisation that could create large hillforts, for communal life and perhaps for protection. There are a wide range of settlements from single farms to small villages. This rural pattern does not appear to change significantly after the Roman Conquest in AD 43. The urbanisation of Dorchester however, covered over anything that remained of the earlier cultures in that area.

Settlements and agricultural production continued to grow during the Romano-British period. Heavier more fertile clay soils in the valleys could be put under more effective ploughs. At the end of this period the occupation of high ground contracted. It has been suggested that Saxon development in Dorset was late, but they certainly had political control of the county by the early eight century. Evidence from land charters shows the beginnings of a parish system that is recognisable today across the Ridgeway area. Woodward (1983) suggests that many of these boundaries were based on even older Bronze Age field systems. Many of the settlements known to us today were also in place at this time, although others have now shrunken or disappeared.

Today's surviving settlements are all concentrated below the ridge,

A typical cottage in the Ridgeway area, built with rubble-stone walls and a thatched roof. The stone probably came from a local source, in this case near Osmington. There was a Purbeck and Portland limestone quarry close by at Poxwell.

RIGHT Many larger buildings would have used local building materials in their construction and restoration works. The Church of St Michael and All Angels at Littlebredy was originally built of rubble-stone and dressed stone walls from the thirteenth century.

BELOW RIGHT A fine example of a local rubble-stone barn at Whitcombe near Broadmayne. This example dates from the mid eighteenth century and has a thatched roof. Restored in 2008, the tower of the former parish church can just be seen behind the barn.

to the north along the valley of the South Winterborne and to the south along the spring line in sheltered combes or valleys.

Their character is often determined by their proximity to water and the nature of the local stone for domestic and community buildings. Portland and Purbeck stone were quarried along the ridge from Portesham to Osmington. The quarries were active from the seventeenth century to their peak in the 1900s. Brick is far less common, with local brickmaking works contributing to garden walls and much later to building around Broadmayne and Dorchester in the nineteenth century. The brickyards closed at the outbreak of the Second World War. Many homes are thatched or roofed with stone slates. In the South Winterborne valley domestic buildings rely on flint, Lower Purbeck stone in rubble (uneven stone) walls and chalk cob. Further east, in Broadmayne for example, there are more brick buildings and clay cob. Portland stone was often used as ashlar, or better quality dressed stone. Finer buildings sometimes have examples of Ham stone windows.

The villages each have a focal point of church and manor. Many of the churches were originally wooden buildings but were rebuilt with stone from 1100 to 1300 AD and often further expanded a century or two later. Many had towers and porches added at this time, funded by the growth of sheep farming and the lucrative wool

ABOVE Bridehead in the mid nineteenth century.

LEFT The pleasing waterfall at Bridehead was created in the 1830s when the River Bride was dammed to form an ornamental lake.

trade. Contemporary writers such as Daniel Defoe (1724) commented on the numbers of sheep grazing the South Dorset Ridgeway. The control of large flocks was helped by the enclosure of large areas of open downland into large rectangular fields from the sixteenth century. On the whole, newly enclosed land was still worked from farmsteads located within villages. Some new buildings were built within the enclosures, often just barns and sheds around a yard that were later abandoned. There are several examples of these along the Ridgeway, as well as farms that continue working today. Hidden in fields and amongst farm buildings are also the remains of many other settlements which have not survived to today.

The area is also home to several large estates and ancient manors. Much of the landscape has been managed by these estates for over a thousand years, from the abbots of Abbotsbury and Cerne to the descendents of families who have lived here for several centuries.

One such estate is Bridehead at the top of the Bride Valley. The valley cuts through the widest part of the Ridgeway at its western end with the River Bride flowing west to the sea at Burton Bradstock. The source of the river is a spring below the chalk of the South Dorset Ridgeway. The top of the valley is occupied by the Bridehead Estate. The manor is listed in the Domesday Book as a possession of Cerne Abbey where it remained until the Dissolution of the Monasteries in 1539. Granted to the Mellor family, a descendent called Robert is said to have built a house at Bridehead in the seventeenth century. This now forms the eastern block of the present house. The estate was purchased by the Williams family in 1798 and the house was largely rebuilt in about 1837. The history of this manor is quite typical apart from the development of a landscaped park dating from the early nineteenth century incorporating a lake, park and the model village of Littlebredy. The park was planted between 1797 and 1814 by Robert Williams and the lake formed in the 1830s by damming the source of the river. Architect Peter Frederick Robertson (1776-1858) worked on the village between 1830 and 1833, followed by Benjamin Ferrey (1810-1880) in 1838. Most of the work was completed by 1842 and little of the layout has changed since.

Another Manor in the valley is that of Kingston Russell which has a curious history. During the reign of Edward I (1272-1307) the village had the right to hold a market and fair, but the chapel was in ruins by the mid eighteenth century and the main settlement moved to north of the A35. Kingston Russell village, with records from 1280, lost its church at the same time.

The South Dorset Ridgeway, once an ancient trackway is crossed

Kingston Russell House. Local tradition says that a coach pulled by four headless horses, driven by a headless coachman, and footman, and containing four headless passengers drives up to the door of the house, stays a moment and then drives away.

by more modern routes joining the settlements on either side of the hill. Some of these follow the route of the old way, for example Bishop's Road to Hardy Monument and at Came Down to White Horse Hill. The most prominent road is now the A354 joining Weymouth to Dorchester. The road follows the approximate line of that constructed by the Roman military in the first century AD. From 1761 the Weymouth, Melcombe Regis & Dorchester Turnpike Trust tidied up the route between Weymouth and Dorchester and the connection with the Great Western Turnpike at Winterbourne Steepleton, the present day B3159. A tollhouse has survived at Martinstown (SY653887). It appears that the roads certainly needed some work: writer Celia Fiennes who travelled from Dorchester to Bridport at the end of the seventeenth century recorded 'The wayes are stony and very narrow'. The Portesham to Winterbourne Abbas Road was created by the

Many of the houses that give Abbotsbury its character were constructed from the local rubble-stone and ashlar originally used to build St Peter's Abbey.

ABBOTSBURY

St Peter's Abbey was first founded in about 1026 as a college for secular canons by Orc a steward to King Canute. In about 1044 it became a Benedictine monastery with great influence over the surrounding area. The village was large and prosperous by Dorset standards. The abbot was granted a weekly market in 1274 which must have flourished as it led to a dispute with the townspeople of Bridport who claimed that theirs was being damaged.

Very little is known of the abbey's earliest buildings as extensive remodelling occurred. The surviving atmospheric buildings and ruins date from the thirteenth and fourteenth centuries. These include the impressive tithe barn, which would have been one of the largest in England. Now partly thatched, it would have originally been roofed in stone.

Dissolved in 1539 the estate was purchased by the Strangways family who still own and manage the area. The Strangways family came to Dorset in about 1500 from Yorkshire, and a descendent was well placed to take advantage of the sale in 1542. The abbey's walls soon found their way into the village; houses such as Abbey House in Church Street is one such example. It dates from the seventeenth century and uses fourteenth century material from the abbey.

The Parish Church of St Nicholas is famous for a Civil War siege and bullet holes are still visible in the pulpit.

short-lived Abbotsbury and Bridport Turnpike Trust in 1777. Further east at Broadmayne, what is known as Chalky Road from the village to the crest of the Ridgeway was created as a carriage road in 1811 as part of an Enclosure Act.

Other villages that lie below the ridge include Abbotsbury, Portesham, Upwey, Bincombe and Sutton Poyntz to the south, Broadmayne and Whitcombe to the north together with the communities along the South Winterborne.

BINCOMBE

The parish of Bincombe provides the South Dorset Ridgeway with evidence of its oldest human inhabitants from 100,000 years ago. Palaeolithic hunter-gatherers used the steep-sided valley and left stone hand axes as evidence of their passing. These can now be seen in the Dorset County Museum. A scattering of flint tools from the end of the last ice age (Mesolithic, 10,000 years ago) found on Bincombe Down, a Neolithic long barrow, many Bronze Age round barrows and the remains of 'Celtic' Fields provide evidence of continual occupation of the valley and hillside.

Bincombe is the only village in the parish, lying at the bottom of the deep valley.

Holy Trinity Church (SY686845) has parts dating from the twelfth century but was heavily restored in 1862. The churchyard witnessed dramatic events in the village's history when in 1801 The York Hussars under the command of the Duke of York were encamped on Bincombe Down. Two soldiers were shot for desertion and buried in the churchyard. The romantic story of one of those soldiers and a local girl was told to Thomas Hardy and became his tale 'The Melancholy Hussar of the German Legion'. There may also be some truth to the assertion that Bincombe Down is the hill that the Grand Old Duke of York marched his 10,000 men up and down in training whilst waiting to do battle with Napoleon. Sadly there are stronger claims from other parts of the country.

BROADMAYNE

Today Broadmayne is a large village lying to the north of the Ridgeway along a busy road. The name comes from the 'Celtic' maen, meaning stone. In the Domesday Book of 1086 several 'maines' are recorded but these are believed to be the settlements of Little Mayne to the west of the current village and Fryermayne to the east. Both have now shrunk to farms and houses with only lumps and bumps in the ground to show the location of former homes and streets. Fryermayne House, built in about 1600 has an association with the Knights Hospitallers on whose manor house site it probably stands.

The medieval community of Broadmayne lies slightly to the north of the present village and the remains of banks, ditches and house platforms can still be seen. The village would have had a strong relationship with the Ridgeway, with the parish boundary extending onto the top of the hill and sheep being grazed. The field name Poor Lot survives, showing poorer villagers had the right to collect wood and gorse for their fires from the ridge. An even earlier Iron Age and Romano British settlement has also been uncovered at Broadmayne along with Bronze Age burials. It may be even be possible that this was the home of a group whose territory was marked by the Neolithic bank barrow.

The medieval growth of the village was fixed around St Martin's Church, which still has some thirteenth century features and a rare south tower completed in the fifteenth century. The church was heavily restored from 1865-6 by John Hicks of Dorchester. His draughtsman was Thomas Hardy, whose drawings survive.

Broadmayne is most widely known for the bricks that were made here, particularly during the nineteenth century. Characteristically speckled, caused by nodules of manganese in the clay, examples of Broadmayne brick can be seen throughout local towns, especially in Dorchester. Production ceased in 1939 when wartime blackout regulations prevented the lighting of kilns. During the Second World War the village became a base for British and US servicemen awaiting embarkation from Weymouth for the D-Day Normandy landings.

PORTESHAM

The village has a Saxon heritage and was once owned by Orc who in 1026 gave his lands to the monastery at Abbotsbury, in whose hands it remained until the Dissolution in 1539. Sometime in the seventeenth century merchant Sir Andrew Riccard purchased the manor and the

LEFT Portesham House, an eighteenth century village house that once belonged to Vice Admiral Sir Thomas Masterman Hardy.

BELOW LEFT The enchanting but small St Bartholomew's Chapel at Corton, near Portesham. Corton was mentioned in Domesday but has shrunk as a settlement to the farmstead there today. A former free chapel, not under the jurisdiction of any Bishop, the medieval building was abandoned as a place of worship in the seventeenth century and used as a thatched barn before being restored and reconsecrated in 1897.

Manor House dates from this time. The Parish Church of St Peter is typical of this area, mainly dating to the fifteenth century with traces of earlier work. The present day village is surrounded by an open field system with the parish's smaller settlements to the east. The villages of Waddon, Little Waddon, Corton and Friar Waddon were once larger and now shrunken to hamlets or just farms. East and West Shilvinghampton are smaller but survive, however three villages with this name were recorded in 1086.

SUTTON POYNTZ

At the base of the steep southern side of the South Dorset Ridgeway a spring to the River Jordan emerges at Sutton Poyntz through a geological fault line. The presence of this spring has perhaps contributed to the existence of people in the area from prehistoric times to today. By the Iron Age the focus of settlement here may have been on the hillfort at nearby Chalbury.

The village gets its name from one of the families who owned the lands in the past. The Poyntz family were only involved in the village for a century (c1275-1375) but their legacy lives on in the name. Over the next 550 years the estate passed through only 4 families, until

1925 when the Welds put everything up for sale. The auction led to a rapid development of the village towards Preston and uphill towards the Ridgeway. Once largely an agricultural community, included within the parish of St Andrew's at Preston, the village soon became the home for people working further afield in nearby Weymouth.

The valley and presence of water made it an ideal location for milling and in the nineteenth century a water turbine house was erected to extract water to feed the growing population of Weymouth. The pumping station still supplies the town today.

UPWEY

The village which lies below the southern slope of the Ridgeway stretches from the former manor of Elwell to Upwey proper, at the Church of St Laurence. The manor at Upwey had no manorial rights, but was part of the property of Salisbury Cathedral. The house was

The attractive mill pond at Sutton Poyntz.

built in 1639 and survives.

A spring is the source of the River Wey and also feeds the spot known as Upwey Wishing Well, which has long been a gathering place for visitors to the area. It is said that George III enjoyed visits here when he stayed in Weymouth. The river provided the power for Upwey Mill, said to be the inspiration for 'Overcombe Mill' in Hardy's *The Trumpet Major*.

West of St Laurence's Church and accessible by public footpath is Windsbatch Quarry. The site is probable medieval and may have provided stone not only for the church but for others locally and in Dorchester. It is known that the Lower Purbeck limestone from here was sent to build the Tower of London during the reign of Edward III (1312-1377).

LEFT Whitcombe church sits amidst fields, and a church has probably stood in this spot since King Athelstan made Whitcombe part of the endowment of Milton Abbey in about 966.

BELOW The development of the villages of Winterbourne Abbas and Steepleton along the line of the South Winterborne. Winterbourne Steepleton is the village at the bottom of the photograph.

WHITCOMBE

Referred to as Widecombe in the Domesday Book in 1086 this shrunken hamlet is remarkable today for the small church that lies in a field beside the road. Fragments of two surviving Saxon crosses suggest an early foundation, with a twelfth century nave. Further developments took place through to the sixteenth century, there are traces of earlier wall paintings. The Dorset dialect poet William Barnes (1801-1886) was rector of Winterborne Came and Whitcombe and preached his first and last sermons here.

WINTERBOURNE ABBAS

In nineteenth century trade directories and gazetteers, Winterbourne Abbas is noted as the source of the South Winterbourne and for the *'Druidical circle and numerous barrows'*. Indeed its proximity to the

RIGHT Winterbourne Steepleton. Originally one of a pair, the beautiful Saxon carving of a Flying Angel would have sat on either side of a rood screen. After spending part of its life secured to the wall outside the church the angel is now safely fixed in the nave.

Nine Stones has long been a claim to fame, but the attractive village is largely built with local flints and the thirteenth century church of St Mary's is of interest because it still contains a rare seventeenth century gallery: most were removed from Dorset churches during the rush to 'tidy-up' churches in the nineteenth century.

Superstition has it that no-one has ever seen the winterbourne break, that is when it is dry one day and wet the next. A local tale, recorded in the 1880's, relates that years before a watch was kept night and day for two weeks. The story goes on that the watchman needed to light his pipe and decided to nip over to Bridehead Lodge for a light. He was gone for three minutes and of course the Winterbourne broke, unseen.

WINTERBOURNE STEEPLETON.

The church of St Michael and All Angels tells an older story of Saxon origins. This small church was once more important than its size would have the visitor believe. Being a Minster Church it housed a community of clergy, serving a wider area than the current parish which probably came into being from the eleventh century. A beautiful carved angel from the late tenth-early eleventh century has survived and can be seen inside the nave. The church is also special in being only one of two in Dorset with a steeple, giving the village its name.

WINTERBORNE ST MARTIN/ MARTINSTOWN

This is the village with two names. Martinstown refers to the village and Winterborne St Martin to the parish, which also included two other settlements long since disappeared.

There are several references to winterbourne settlements in the Domesday Book, but some of these refer to villages along the River (North) Winterbourne (a tributary of the Dorset Stour) as well. The narrow strip of land on either side of the river would have been ideal to set up a home. As with many valley villages there is a just a single street, with a 'back lane' that is now a footpath. To the west, the remains of the village of Rew can be seen as lumps and bumps in a field along side the winterbourne. To the east the village of Ashton has shrunk to two farms below the ramparts of Maiden Castle. The people farmed the land around the valley, using the Ridgeway for

Martinstown sheepwash can be found beside the village public house.

THE SOUTH WINTERBORNE
Alison Turnock

Most chalk rivers have winterbourne headwaters at the top end of the river, which become dry during the summer and early autumn and only flow again when recharged by winter rains.

The source of the South Winterborne is the 'Wherry Pit' spring at Winterbourne Abbas. It then runs for approximately 14 km through a succession of winterbourne villages including Winterbourne Steepleton, Winterbornes Monkton, Herringston and Came before joining the River Frome near West Stafford.

The winterbourne would originally have followed a natural meandering route. In many places, the gravelly bed of the winterbourne was considered an ideal route for a path and roads were built along the course of the river which was dry in the summer. Much of the current route of the river has been straightened and reinforced with concrete and water pumped in to enable parts of the stream to run year round.

Winterbournes are harsh environments ecologically speaking – species that live in them have to be able to survive both drought and flood. A number of species have adapted to enable them to cope with these extremes. One of these is a mayfly so rare it has no common name – *Paraleptophlebia werneri*. This is found in the middle stretches of the stream that are truly winterbourne. It survives by laying drought-resistant eggs in the stream bed, which lie dormant during the dry months and hatch when the river is flowing. Although winterbournes can hold fish if they flow for long enough each year, they do not contain as many fish as a permanently flowing river. This makes them attractive habitats for frogs, newts and toads, which breed in the early spring in winterbourne pools

grazing their stock. There are good examples of surviving open fields and strip lynchets at nearby Winterbourne Steepleton. The residents of Martinstown called the Ridgeway 'The Sea Wall', perhaps viewing it as a barrier to the coast beyond.

Martinstown is fortunate to retain its nineteenth century sheepwash; another wash survives in the river at Broadmayne. The value of sheep farming to the local economy is provided by evidence of a charter granted to Winterborne St Martin by Henry II for a Market and Fair on St Martin's Day, 11th November. The fair was later moved to the 23rd November and continued until 1978. Daniel Defoe described Martinstown Fair in 1720 as 'the greatest fair for sheep that this nation can show'.

The South Winterborne flowing through fields at Winterborne Herringston.

and are relatively safe from predation by fish.

A string of villages ran through the valley during medieval times. Some are still villages, others survive as farms or simply the humps and bumps of deserted settlements in fields near the river, such as the site of the medieval village of Winterbourne Farringdon. Clues to their origins can be seen in villages today, with parish churches generally situated on their original medieval plots and the survival of property boundaries and street layouts. Surviving medieval and later farm houses, barns and other agricultural structures show the importance of farming to valley life over the centuries.

More recently, the Dorset Winterbournes Project has been working with local communities and organisations to increase awareness of the importance of these ephemeral streams. One aim is to restore where possible the stream to a more natural course. At Winterborne Came, where the river had been straightened and deepened, it has been returned to a more sinuous course. Surveys have shown that this is much more attractive to wildlife, with rare species being recorded only months after the work was completed.

FARMING

'...here it was that they told me, that there were 600,000 sheep fed on the downs, within six miles of the town; that is, six miles every way, which is twelve miles in diameter, and thirty six miles in circumference. This I say, I was told, I do not affirm it to be true; but when I viewed the country round, I confess I could not but incline to believe it.'

Daniel Defoe 1724

A combe near Portesham. Remains of strip lynchets can be seen on the left. Across the valley the outline of older fields can also be seen.

The earliest agricultural marks in the Ridgeway's landscape are the so-called 'Celtic' field systems dating from the prehistoric to Roman periods. A fine example can be seen looking south-west from Bronkham Hill, covering the ridge east of Black Down Barn. Small, square or rectangular fields, their boundaries are marked by raised ridges. These formed by soil creep over generations of ploughing, the soil banking up around boundary hedges or walls that no longer exist.

These field-edge ridges are known as 'lynchets', but more widely known in this part of Dorset are 'strip lynchets'. Largely, the latter weren't caused by the action of the plough but by serious spadework. Possibly a sign of excess manpower or desperation to intensify food production, strip lynchets are medieval terraces. Terracing has two effects: increasing the total surface area of a slope, and enabling oxen to plough land otherwise too steep. These terraces were probably not in use for long as the population was dramatically reduced by the Black Death shortly after their construction – it is thought the disease entered Britain through the nearby port of Melcombe Regis in 1347.

Excellent strip lynchets can be seen in Coombe Valley (SY693839), immediately west of Chalbury Hillfort.

About thirty per cent of the population died in the Black Death, this meant fewer mouths to feed and fewer hands to tend the plough. Sheep farming became widespread, it was (and still is) a less labour-intensive method of farming than arable. Wool was a lucrative product; some of the wool wealth was invested in church building – Martinstown's grand church, mostly fifteenth century, was funded from these riches.

Sheep have been regularly 'folded' on the Ridgeway's downlands since that time – some of the great wildflower grasslands in the area are a legacy of this longevity of grazing. Arguably the greatest landscape change since the creation of the medieval terrace was brought about by agricultural intensification in the mid twentieth century.

The combined effects of mechanisation, food security concerns in the two World Wars and the European Common Agricultural Policy led to an expansion of grain-growing. The Ridgeway's generally light soils suit barley and to some extent wheat on the land that can be ploughed; still evident in some areas is the sharp line between the 'improved', greener grass or arable of the broader hilltops and the wildflower-rich 'unimproved' land of the steep slopes.

Policy changes have led to the introduction of incentives to

RIGHT Autumn ploughing at Holcombe on the ridge above Broadmayne.

BELOW Folding sheep on Dorset downland, a typical sight from the Middle Ages until well into the twentieth century using locally made hurdles as temporary fencing.

One remarkable survival is the Celtic field system in the Valley of the Stones.

introduce environmental enhancements to farming – the first was the Environmentally Sensitive Area scheme, covering part of the Ridgeway area from 1993. This scheme followed others that have covered the whole area, enabling changes such as stone wall reconstruction, reverting arable to grassland, enhancement with wildflowers and conservation grazing.

Policy and market developments have a great influence on farming changes. Farming will continue to adapt to meet demands and opportunities as farming families and businesses find ways to make a living from the land. Influences are varied: the increasing global population, shortages of fossil fuels and the demand for renewable energy may all leave their marks.

WILDLIFE

David Emery, Jon Campbell and John Newbould

The South Dorset Ridgeway's more natural habitats are largely chalk grassland or downland, except on the high ground around Hardy Monument where the sand and gravel geology gives rise to a stretch of acid heathland with heather and bilberry.

Classically chalk downland provides the home for a rich variety of wildlife, particularly wild flowers and butterflies, and the Ridgeway is no exception. To the north there are large open fields of intensive agriculture, which inevitably reduces the variety of wildlife. However, the steeper slopes still retain a diverse range of wildlife. Even the patches of scrub, which are often viewed as an eyesore against rolling grass downland, give cover to a large variety of native species.

Chalk grassland when sympathetically managed supports a wide range of wild flowers; the more common ones to look out for include small scabious and greater knapweed as well as, in favoured places, good numbers of pyramidal orchids. Another common family of wild flowers are the vetches, particularly bird's-foot trefoil (called 'eggs and

Pyramidal orchids are found on the chalky grassland of the South Dorset Ridgeway and even in some roadside verges. The plant gets its name from the conical or pyramid shape to the pink or purple spikes of flowers from June to August.

bacon' because of the red-tinged yellow flowers) and horseshoe vetch, which are food plants for a wide range of butterflies. In some places the grassland has been invaded by rank tor-grass but elsewhere, such as along the Bincombe Bumps, the finer chalk grassland has flowers such as harebell and autumn lady's-tresses.

Along many parts of the Ridgeway butterflies such as common blue, Adonis blue, small heath, dark green fritillary and wall brown can be seen on a regular basis but they all have limited flight seasons so you can't see everything at once. The Lulworth skipper may be found from Sutton Poyntz to Osmington as well as the more common skippers. Day-flying moths can often be seen, such as the bright red

LEFT The brown hare lives on the Ridgeway throughout the year, but is most likely to be seen in spring and early summer.

BELOW LEFT The buzzard is recognisable for its rounded head and tail, broad wings and soaring, circling flight. They are common along the Ridgeway, often appearing in pairs or groups.

BELOW The kestrel can often be seen hovering over farmland and at the sides of roads. It has a long tail and narrow wings and is easy to identify.

Walkers on the Ridgeway will hear the skylark long before they see one. With nests well hidden on the ground the birds hang suspended overhead in a territorial display that can last for as long as five minutes.

The numbers of now protected corn bunting have declined in recent years and their presence is patchy in many areas.

The meadow pipit is the most common songbird in upland areas and can be found along the Ridgeway throughout the year.

The linnet is slightly smaller than a sparrow. Males have chestnut backs and grey heads and during the breeding season they develop a striking pinkish-crimson crown and breast. They can be found on farmland in the summer.

Two of the butterflies found on the Ridgeway include the most common of the fritillaries, the dark green fritillary, and one of Britain's rarest, the Adonis blue.

and black six-spot burnet and in June the burnet companion.

Perhaps the birds most commonly noted along the Ridgeway in spring are the skylark and meadow pipit. Wherever the ploughed fields break up the dominant pattern of downland grass, a walker is likely to come across both these small brown birds. In late March especially, the first energetic singing of the skylark above his territory is a characteristic of this landscape. Soon afterwards early migrants, like the European wheatear, can be seen by rock outcrops or perched on drystone walls along the Ridgeway tops.

The once-common but now quite rare corn bunting is resident along the higher contours, perhaps spreading out from its local breeding stronghold around Maiden Castle. During the summer months good numbers of linnet with its flushed red breast and the canary-yellow coloured yellowhammer with its wheezing song (long described as 'a-little-bit-of-bread-and-no-cheese') are usually seen.

Even in winter, there are still interesting birds to be seen in the Ridgeway landscape, taking advantage of its food resources and relative remoteness at this time of year. Instead of breeding birds there are now regular winter visitors like the Scandinavian thrushes, redwing and the larger fieldfare, and smaller numbers of lapwing and golden plovers can be seen on sheltered fields on the lower slopes, especially during hard frosts. Throughout the year sizeable numbers of the most common birds of prey, the buzzard and kestrel, as well as raven can usually be seen flying overhead.

Finally the more common larger mammals such as roe deer, fox and rabbit can be seen by the keen observer along the field boundaries, whilst hares are occasionally spotted in the adjacent arable fields.

INSPIRATIONAL RIDGEWAY

THOMAS HARDY AND THE SOUTH DORSET RIDGEWAY

Tony Fincham

Thomas Hardy (1840-1928), the great Wessex poet and novelist, was a lover of high isolated hill-tops and ridges. Foremost amongst which were the South Dorset Downs which separated his heartland of Egdon Heath and Casterbridge (Dorchester) from the seaside delights of Budmouth (Weymouth) and the wild Channel coast, where 'hill-hid tides throb throe on throe' (*Weathers*). Hardy advocated the benefits of Ridgeway paths in *Wessex Heights* (1896), often considered to be his greatest poem:

> There are some heights in Wessex, shaped as if by a kindly hand
> For thinking, dreaming, dying on, and at crises when I stand,
> Say, on Ingpen Beacon eastward, or on Wylls-Neck westwardly,
> I seem where I was before my birth, and after death may be.

Hill-top routes such as the South Dorset Ridgeway were a final citadel against 'the devices and desires of this world', a place of retreat and a place of communion with both nature and the inner self – the expression of an instinctual need to escape to a place where 'mind-chains do not clank' because 'one's next neighbour is the sky'; a place

And the coomb and the upland
Foliage-crowned,
Ancient chalk-pit, milestone, rills in the grass-flat
Stroked by the light,
Seemed but a ghost-like gauze, and no substantial
Meadow or mound.
Thomas Hardy, In Front of the Landscape

Much of what we understand today as 'landscape' is largely shaped by art and literature and our perception of the Ridgeway is no exception. The area has long provided inspiration for writers and artists who have lived close by, in particular Thomas Hardy (1840-1928) who used the setting as a backdrop to some well known tales. In 2009 a contemporary art exhibition at Dorset County Museum brought together a number of visual artists for the first time, influenced by this landscape.

Writers and artists all invest a powerful and emotional involvement with their subject matter. Sometimes they distort the image, making a decision about what to include or exclude from the environment around them. For writers this might mean referring to real events out of time, for a visual artist excluding form in favour of colour and texture – laying down and removing layers of material in reflection of natural processes over time. However the landscape inspires the artist the response is individual and can influence our own perception of an area we feel already familiar with or have yet to know.

Thomas Hardy was well-known locally for riding his bicycle.

short story *The Melancholy Hussar of the German Legion*, both of which are set in the opening years of the nineteenth century, at a time when it was believed that Napoleon was planning to invade England via the Dorset coast. King George's troops were encamped on the downs above Overcombe (Sutton Poyntz).

The narrator of *The Melancholy Hussar*, which is based upon actual events which occurred in 1801, climbs the Ridgeway noting that:

> Here stood the camp; here are distinct traces of the banks thrown up for the horses of the cavalry, and spots where the midden-heaps lay are still to be observed. At night, when I walk across the lonely place, it is impossible to avoid hearing, amid the scourings of the wind over the grass-bents and thistles, the old trumpet and bugle calls, the rattle of the halters; to help seeing rows of spectral tents and the impedimenta of the soldiery. From within the canvases come guttural syllables of foreign tongues, and broken songs of the fatherland; for they were mainly regiments of the King's German Legion that slept round the tent-poles hereabout at that time.

Anne Garland, the heroine of *The Trumpet-Major* visits the camp, climbing to the summit of the tumulus on East Hill (158 metres) – on 'a clear day' with 'a little wind stirring' one of the best view-points in the county:

> The eye of any observer who cared for such things swept over the wave-washed town, and the bay beyond, and the Isle, with its pebble bank, lying on the sea to the left of these, like a great crouching animal tethered to the mainland. On the extreme east of the marine horizon, St. Aldhelm's Head closed the scene, the sea to the southward of that point glaring like a mirror under the sun. Inland could be seen Badbury Rings, where a beacon had been recently erected; and nearer, Rainbarrow, on Egdon Heath, where another stood: farther to the left Bulbarrow, where there was yet another. Not far from this came Nettlecombe Tout; to the

where in William Wordsworth's phrase 'the heavy and weary weight / Of all this unintelligible world / Is lightened'.

The countryside of the South Dorset Ridgeway features most prominently in Hardy's novel *The Trumpet-Major* (1880) and the west, Dogberry Hill, and Black'on near to the foreground, the beacon thereon being built of furze faggots thatched with straw, and standing on the spot where the monument now raises its head.

Following the Ridgeway into the next field with its sheer escarpment, Anne encounters a party of workmen 'cutting out a huge picture of the king on horseback in the earth of the hill. The King's head is as big as our mill-pond and his body as big as our garden'. Further east from White Horse Hill, the Ridgeway leads to (P)oxwell, where Squire Derriman's manor house, depicted in the final stages of decay in *The Trumpet-Major*, is now restored to its original early seventeenth century glory.

Heading westward from Anne's view point, the Ridgeway traverses West Hill, then circumvents Green Hill before ascending the slopes of Bincombe Hill; Hardy describes how:

Here stretch the downs, high and breezy and green, absolutely unchanged since those eventful days. A plough has never disturbed the turf, and the sod that was uppermost then is uppermost now!

The Hussars' graves at Bincombe.

This assertion remains true, for Bincombe, hidden behind its protective knoll, has – unlike its neighbours – managed to keep the modern world at bay. It remains a jewel – a tiny tranquil piece of old Dorset, where the Melancholy Hussar and his fellow deserter are buried at the rear of the churchyard.

West from Bincombe lies Upwey. Here at the junction of the Ridgeway and the straight Old Roman Road, the local population (Anne Garland included) gathered to catch a glimpse of King George III and the Royal carriages on their way to Budmouth, in an account by Hardy based upon contemporary newspaper reports. The old road can still be followed – a chalky byway through the trees leading down to that original 'good inn', The Ship. In *Under the Greenwood Tree* Dick Dewy rested his horses here 'going and coming' and this is where,

on that memorable Sunday he and Fancy became engaged. Hardy also was inclined to break his journey here:

Sweet cyder is a great thing,
A great thing to me,
        Spinning down to Weymouth town
        By Ridgway thirstily,
        And maid and mistress summoning
Who tend the hostelry:
        O cyder is a great thing,
        A great thing to me!

In addition to King George, one other real historical figure appears in *The Trumpet-Major*, namely Captain (later Admiral) Hardy whose solid Victorian memorial, erected on the crest of Black Down,

The village of Upwey nestles in the lee of the Ridgeway's southern escarpment around the Parish Church of St Laurence. The church's late fifteenth century tower can clearly be seen.

dominates the skyline ahead for the walker heading west from Upwey. Without climbing the tower there are still fine views over the Fleet towards Budmouth and Hardy's Isle of Slingers (Portland). Below Black Down, beside the road junction in nearby Portesham still stands unchanged 'the old-fashioned house which was the family residence of the Hardys'.

Hardy would have kept to the Ridgeway heading for Abbotsbury Hill, one mile west of the village, where on a clear windy day can be found the best views of all, over Chesil Beach and the Isle of Slingers. For Hardy 'mind-chains do not clank where one's next neighbour is the sky' – thus liberated:

> So I am found on Ingpen Beacon, or on Wylls-Neck to the west,
> Or else on homely Bulbarrow, or little Pilsdon Crest,
> Where men have never cared to haunt, nor women have walked with me,
> And ghosts then keep their distance; and I know some liberty.

AN ARTIST'S RIDGEWAY
John Walker

With the whole of the outstandingly beautiful county of Dorset to mine for motifs what's so special about the Ridgeway? As a painter I look at the landscape with a poet's eye and in my case an unrepentantly Romantic eye. For me nowhere else in the county does the spirit of place make itself so evident; nowhere else does the landscape offer such an easy escape into the numinous; nowhere else offers such opportunities for the translation of observed reality into an image. The light varies from soft grey to a strong southern glare and, of importance to the English, one is always within sight and/or sound of the sea.

People of sensitivity identify themselves in the landscape and every generation of artists, disregarding fashion and critics, have felt and communicated this attachment through their work. For the less susceptible majority only in times of acute stress are our landscape and historic monuments suddenly revealed as precious and able to encapsulate the deep taproot of our national identity.

How to portray the spirit of this landscape? Thomas Hardy neatly expressed the approach I espouse:

'Nature is played out as a Beauty, but not as a Mystery ... I don't want to see original realities ... I want to see the deeper reality underlying the scenic, the expression of what are sometimes called abstract imaginings'.

I find the Ridgeway is where an expression of this 'deeper reality' can be most readily extracted from the concrete world.

The ancient monuments are an inevitable feature of a landscape of the imagination. On a summer's day they can conjure-up a mythic, Arcadian world where you might encounter Pan himself. In a mist the weathered rock of the Hell Stone or the Grey Mare and her Colts, or encountering a wind-threshed thorn bush or a racing hare, you can connect with the mysterious, unlettered world of our prehistoric forebears. In this timeless landscape of the mind, in the company of crops and animals, you can feel intimately in touch with the world we have inherited from our most remote ancestors.

However the continuous agricultural activity serves as a reminder that this is very much a living landscape shaped by generations of hard work. Consider the labour, no doubt winter work, in the construction of the drystone walls: the visual delight of the place has been hard-won.

Pattern and colour are of central importance in my work. The pattern of masonry, the pattern of drystone walls, the patterns

Maiden Castle by John Walker. The painting makes use of many of John's favourite motifs including the historic landscape, the stone walls and the running hare.

that agriculture and sheep sculpt, the unwonted colour harmony of the rusted corrugated-iron roof of a barn next to a field of kale. All coalesce into a patchwork of disparate textures and colours stitched together with stone, each defining the flow, and emphasising the shape, of the land. These are what make the Ridgeway still such an amazing and diverse place. My aim is to touch hands, as it were, with those, past, present and future, who are sensible to the spirit of this special place.

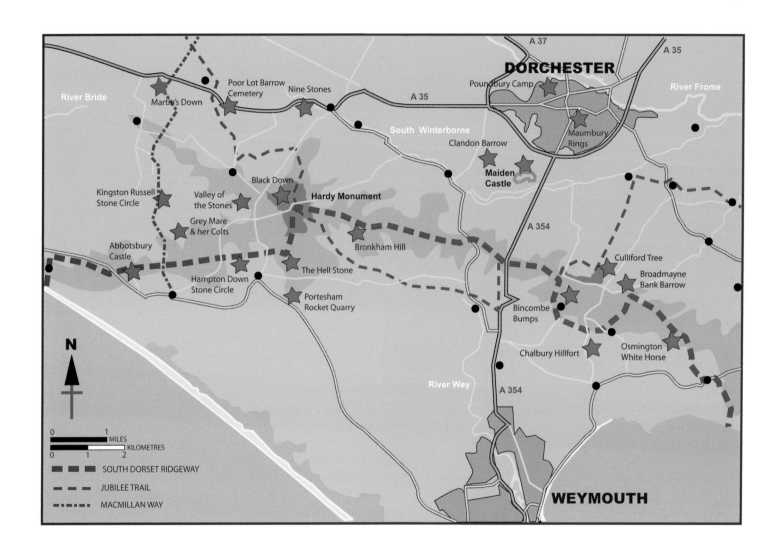

Map legend:

- ▬ ▬ ▬ SOUTH DORSET RIDGEWAY
- - - - JUBILEE TRAIL
- -·-·- MACMILLAN WAY

Labels on map:

River Bride
River Frome
DORCHESTER
A 37
A 35
Poundbury Camp
Poor Lot Barrow Cemetery
Nine Stones
Martin's Down
South Winterborne
Maumbury Rings
Clandon Barrow
Maiden Castle
Kingston Russell Stone Circle
Black Down
Hardy Monument
Valley of the Stones
Grey Mare & her Colts
A 354
Bronkham Hill
Abbotsbury Castle
The Hell Stone
Culliford Tree
Hampton Down Stone Circle
Broadmayne Bank Barrow
Portesham Rocket Quarry
Bincombe Bumps
Chalbury Hillfort
Osmington White Horse
River Wey
A 354
N
0 1 MILES
0 1 2 KILOMETRES
WEYMOUTH

GAZETTEER

Abbotsbury Castle (SY555866)

Abbotsbury Castle is an Iron Age hillfort situated in a prominent position on the South Dorset Ridgeway overlooking the coastline. A triangular-shaped enclosure covers about 1.8 hectares. Three sides were defended by two ramparts with the south-east corner defences consisting of four. A large Bronze Age round barrow sits in the south-west corner. There are only a few more Bronze Age barrows to be seen to the west of this point.

The hillfort's position offers unrivalled views inland across the Bride Valley and east to Hardy Monument and Black Down. Below you can see the village of Abbotsbury and the remains of the medieval abbey founded in 1026. Much of the land around was held by the abbot until the Dissolution of the Monasteries in 1539 when the estate was purchased by Giles Strangways, whose descendents still own much of the surrounding countryside. The views of St Catherine's Chapel, still a site of pilgrimage, and Chesil Bank to Portland are unequalled along the south coast.

The hillfort is located along the route of the South Dorset Ridgeway National Trail.

Martin's Down (SY572912)

This area forms the western end of the South Dorset Ridgeway. An extraordinary Neolithic bank barrow can clearly be seen from the

Portland from near Abbotsbury Castle. The Fleet lagoon and the Chesil Bank lie beyond St Catherine's Chapel.

A35, running north-west to south-east. Known as Long Bredy bank barrow, the long, narrow mound visible today is 197 metres long, 20 metres wide and reaches a height of 1.8 metres. There is an interesting V-shaped groove cut through the barrow, the reason for which is unclear. Like the other bank barrows along the Ridgeway at Maiden Castle and Broadmayne, its use is uncertain. Constructed around 4000 BC, it could mark the territorial boundary of a group of local people. It has also been suggested that bank barrows in Dorset mimic the form of Chesil Bank. Martin's Down may have had a significant

ceremonial function, perhaps related to its position near the source of the winterbourne and the proximity of a cursus at the eastern end. These long narrow rectangular earthworks are usually defined by a bank and ditch and are presumed to have had a ceremonial function. Evidence shows that the area around the bank barrow continued to have significance for the local population for over a thousand years and was used as a focal point for later burial mounds in the Bronze Age, 2000 years later.

Access to the barrow is by way of a footpath from the A35 to Long Barrow Farm (SY571913)

Kingston Russell Stone Circle (SY578878)

Stone circles are rare in Dorset and this is the largest of the three in the Ridgeway area. It is about 30 metres in diameter but with all 18 stones lying down it can be easy to miss when the surrounding grass is long. Its situation on top of a prominent spur of the Ridgeway at Tenant's Hill provides good views over the Bride Valley to the north and Abbotsbury hillfort and the coast to the south-west, and must have been a place of deep significance for the people who constructed it. The circle has been dated to the Late Neolithic or Early Bronze Age and is of a similar date to other stone circles nearby. The stones are a sandstone conglomerate known as sarsen and probably came from the Valley of the Stones about a mile away. They vary in size from 2

The Grey Mare and her Colts. There are four massive sarsen stones at the front of the mound, with a fifth stone lying to one side, all probably originating from the Valley of the Stones.

metres by 0.5 metres to 1 metre by 0.3 metres, although partial burial may mean some of the stones are significantly larger. It is suggested that many of the stones may not be in their original positions; an account of 1815 records one stone to the south as still standing.

Nearby on Tenant's Hill is a Bronze Age earthwork enclosure and medieval dewpond located amid a field system.

The stone circle lies at the centre of a network of footpaths, including the Macmillan Way, and is in the guardianship of English Heritage.

The Grey Mare and her Colts (SY584871)

This Neolithic burial monument is a well preserved example of a chambered long barrow. It has a rectangular mound, lying on a north-west – south-east line and is 24m long. Probably built from around 3800 BC the barrow would have been used for a few generations by a family who lived close by, perhaps farming below the ridge in what is now Gorwell. It was constructed in an open area of chalk woodland on a spur of the ridge that offers fine views of the surrounding coastline. The mound can also been seen clearly from the surrounding hills. Unlike many other long barrows in the Ridgeway area it has survived partly because of the use of stone construction materials rather than wood. Other long barrows have been ploughed out. The mound was excavated in the early

ABOVE Poor Lot Barrow Cemetery straddles both sides of the now busy A35.

LEFT The valley train of sarsen stones in the Valley of the Stones.

nineteenth century when pottery and human remains were found.

The long barrow can easily be seen from footpaths close by (SY585871).

Poor Lot Barrow Cemetery (SY588907)

Winterbourne Poor Lot is a large and impressive Bronze Age barrow cemetery with at least 44 barrows including examples of bell barrows, disc barrows and bowl barrows. The cemetery lies on either side of the A35 but many barrows have been ploughed out and can no longer be seen. The focal point of the cemetery lies on the southern side of the road, in the winterbourne valley bottom, which in itself is somewhat unusual. It is clearly visible from the surrounding hilltops, however.

The site is on private land but the Jubilee Trail passes close by, crossing the A35 at (SY590608). The site is in the guardianship of English Heritage.

Valley of the Stones (SY595880)

The valley is a National Nature Reserve, recognised for a train of sarsen stones and a wide range of unimproved grassland types, uncommon lichens, mosses, liverworts and scarce butterflies.

The sarsen valley train or blockstream is a natural feature dating from the end of the last Ice Age. The deposits of pebbly clay, sand and Bagshot Beds that lay on top of the chalk hilltop gradually fragmented and reformed, travelling downhill under freeze and thaw 'periglacial' conditions. The sarsens in the upper valley are typically conglomerates of flints in a sandy matrix, whilst those in the lower valley are mostly of sandstone. Some stones look like they have been arranged in circles but these are unlikely to be prehistoric sites. However, the sarsens from this valley were definitely removed and used for circles and standing stones elsewhere. They survive across the Ridgeway in historic monuments, churches and houses. It is likely that henge monuments constructed further away used timber, as the stone must have been extremely difficult to move great distances.

The valley is also remarkable for the considerable remains of a Celtic field system that covers its slopes. The term 'Celtic' carries no significant meaning; these small rectangular fields may date from any time between the middle Bronze Age to the Roman period. Arable farming was well established by the Mid Bronze Age and large planned blocks of fields were laid out along the same line regardless of the slope. Here it is in a north-west – south-east alignment. There are other examples of these early fields that survived the growth of arable

Hampton Down Stone Circle: blink and you could miss it!.

farming during the Middle Ages around Littlebredy and Portesham, especially on steeper slopes. Within the Valley of the Stones and neighbouring Crow Hill there is also evidence of hut platforms, suggesting that the farmers lived close by.

The Valley of the Stones is open access; a footpath runs through the valley from Littlebredy Farm (SY595882) to Bishops Road (SY601874).

Hampton Down Stone Circle (SY596865)

This small circle on the ridge above Portesham has been greatly altered over its life. Originally constructed around 2000 BC it is made from local sarsen stones. The circle was probably moved in the seventeenth

The Hell Stone. Local tradition says that the devil flung the stones from Portland during a game of quoits.

century to make way for a banked hedge. A photograph from 1908 shows 16 stones which were still there in 1939. By 1964 this had grown to 28 stones. An excavation a year later revealed that many of the stones were in the wrong place and the circle was originally sited further to the west. The monument was restored into its current form, a 6 metre diameter ellipse with 10 stones, on the correct site.

In the eighteenth century John Hutchins recorded another stone site close by on Portesham Hill. There were four upright stones about two feet high, but one was broken off. A local rhyme declares:

'Jeffrey and Jone

And their little dog Denty, and Edy alone'

These stones probably disappeared as a result of field clearance for farming or could have been used in a local building. From the medieval period onwards many other stone monuments were taken from fields in this way.

The circle is located along the route of the South Dorset Ridgeway National Trail, part of the South West Coast Path National Trail.

The Hell Stone (SY606867)

This Neolithic chambered long barrow sits on a spur of the Ridgeway on Portesham Hill. Although constructed at a similar time to the Grey Mare and her Colts and orientated in the same direction, north-west to south-east, its history could not be more different. In 1866 a group of antiquarians reconstructed the stone chamber at the front of the long earthen mound into a style reminiscent of a portal dolmen further to the south-west. These take the form of a chamber bounded by three or four large upright stones supporting a large capstone over the top. The barrow now resembles this with nine upright sarsen stones supporting a capstone. A drawing from 1790 by S.H. Grimm shows the capstone supported by one or two uprights, tilting to the south with another stone to the north and recumbent stones to south and south-west. Hutchins, writing in the 1770s, comments that the stones were used by shepherds as a shelter.

The Hell Stone can be reached from by way of a permissive path from the South Dorset Ridgeway National Trail at (SY605868).

Portesham Rocket Quarry (SY610859)

The geology underlying the Ridgeway from here to Poxwell includes beds of Portland and Purbeck Limestone. There are several small quarries all along this route that have been used for building materials and limeburning from at least the twelfth century. Limekilns survive above West Bexington (SY540870), Abbotsbury (SY587858) and at Portesham Quarry.

Stone from the Portesham or Rocket Quarry was used to build Abbotsbury Abbey and Athelhampton House near Puddletown. It was also used locally in domestic and church buildings. At some time it closed but re-opened in the 1840s to provide the materials to build the Hardy Monument. In 1887 a siding of the Abbotsbury Railway was connected to the quarry by way of an inclined tramway, the route of which is now followed by a modern farm track. The quarry closed in 1928 and is now recognised as a Regionally Important Geological Site (RIGS), a place recognised for its geological interest. Within the quarry it is possible to see the remains of a fossilised tree (see page 15).

Access to the quarry is open and can be reached by a footpath between Winters Lane and Portesham Farm. The quarry is cared for by the Dorset Important Geological Sites Group (DIGS).

The Nine Stones. In local folklore the stones are also known as the Devil's Nine Stones, representing the Devil, his wife and family.

Nine Stones (SY611904)

This is certainly one of the most intriguing stone circles in the UK. It is small, about 8 metres across, and located in a river valley as opposed to the more usual exposed hill top. Its proximity to the South Winterborne chalk stream may explain its location and its significance to the people of the Late Neolithic or Early Bronze Age who constructed it. The sarsen stones probably came from the Valley of the Stones. The circle was first recorded in the seventeenth century by antiquarian John Aubrey. The site was also visited by another pioneering antiquarian, William Stukeley, in 1723 and has seen little

The Hardy Monument – at 22 metres high there are 84 steps inside. Inset is a portrait of Vice Admiral Sir Thomas Masterman Hardy, Nelson's captain of HMS *Victory* at the Battle of Trafalgar, and the person the tower was built to commemorate.

change since. In local folklore the stones are also known as the Devil's Nine Stones, representing the Devil, his wife and family. They are also known as naughty children who were turned to stone after playing a game of 'five stones' on a Sunday. The stones are also believed to 'dance at 3.00pm on certain days'.

John Aubrey also described another circle about half a mile to the west but this has since been destroyed. Observant drivers on the A35 may spot the Broadstone, a standing stone which was originally 2 metres high. It is now semi-buried in the roadside verge heading towards the west and Bridport.

The circle is looked after by English Heritage and is situated alongside the busy A35. Parking is possible at the Little Chef close by and you can reach the stones by way of a permissive path through the field beside the main road.

Black Down (SY612875)

This area around the Hardy Monument landmark is rare for the South Dorset Ridgeway in being mainly heathland. Barrows have long been hidden under forestry plantation and bracken. Other more recent buildings have also been forgotten. The site of a Second World War Auxiliary Unit Outstation built in 1940 to 1941 still needs to be rediscovered. An older rectangular platform alongside the Portesham to Winterbourne Road (SY603880) also remains a mystery. Identified as a Roman signal station, there is some debate about it being an earlier enclosure. But the most significant feature on this site is the

Hardy Monument itself.

The tower was built in memory of Vice Admiral Sir Thomas Masterman Hardy who was born close by in 1769 and grew up in Portesham. Not to be confused with the writer, this Hardy was captain of HMS *Victory* when Nelson was fatally wounded as they paced the decks together at Trafalgar. Following his death in Greenwich in 1839 a scheme was hatched to remember this local hero. The monument was designed by Arthur Dyke Troyte-Acland and built in 1844 of stone from Rocket Quarry by Henry Goddard of Bridport.

When the monument can clearly be seen from Dorchester, bear in mind this traditional rhyme

'When Hardy's Monument is plainly seen

There'll soon be heavy rain I ween'

Footpaths cross Black Down to either side of the Winterborne St Martin Road. Both the South Dorset Ridgeway National Trail and Jubilee Trail pass through. The Hardy Monument is now in the care of the National Trust. When the tower is open visitors can climb the 84 steps inside for the wonderful views from the top.

Bronkham Hill (SY623872)

The South Dorset Ridgeway provides one of the densest concentrations of Bronze Age funerary monuments in southern England, and the cemetery at Bronkham Hill is perhaps one of the most spectacular groups of barrows on the ridge. The group runs for about a mile along the narrow top of the hill and includes four bell barrows and one double bowl barrow. The appearance of these mounds along the skyline signalled a change in society from around 2400 BC. The spread of bronze making technology, and the trend for individual burials, often alongside a pottery beaker, has left us with an incredible landscape of gentle bumps. At Bronkham Hill however, the

One of the distinct features of the South Dorset Ridgeway is the dry stone walls that mark the field and parish boundaries. At Bronkham Hill some of the boundaries are made up of vertical slabs of local limestone, which could themselves be an ancient feature.

bumps are accompanied by hollows: a natural phenomenon known as dolines. Also called shake holes and sink holes, the dolines are formed when a patch of chalk underneath the top layer of sands and gravels is dissolved. This continues today and many of the holes have been filled with scrap and rubble to protect livestock. The overlying soil here is poor and the area is used for grazing. Its unsuitability for the plough has inevitably helped these monuments survive into the twenty-first century.

Standing on top of one of the larger barrows the views from here are extraordinary. On a clear day, the coastline of southern England from The Needles on the Isle of Wight to Start Point in Devon is clearly visible. The Ridgeway west to Abbotsbury hillfort and east to Purbeck can also be easily appreciated.

Bronkham Hill is an open access area along the South Dorset Ridgeway National Trail.

Clandon (SY656890) and Lanceborough Barrows (SY666892)

These two large bowl barrows both lie apart from the South Dorset Ridgeway in prominent positions. Clandon Barrow, near Martinstown, is one of the few in the Ridgeway area whose excavation was recorded. The importance of this site is now recognised, although possibly not fully understood. Lanceborough Barrow near Maiden Castle is part of group of monuments which includes other round barrows and a linear earthwork, a cross dyke (a bank) which runs across the ridge, rather than along it. The dyke may have been built as a field boundary or to protect the barrows in the medieval period. All the monuments here have been damaged by ploughing. In the 1844 Tithe Map the adjacent open field is called Lanceborough or Great Barrow Furlong.

Clandon Barrow lies on private property alongside a bridleway between Maiden Castle and Martinstown. The barrow is best viewed from Stevens Farm (SY648892), Grove Hill Bottom (SY646884) and the South Dorset Ridgeway itself (SY656866).

Lanceborough Barrow lies on private land but is easily visible from Maiden Castle and the surrounding area.

A contrast in seasons.
ABOVE The southern ramparts of Maiden Castle in winter, looking west.
RIGHT Clandon Barrow in high summer from a footpath south of Martinstown, below Grove Hill.

Maiden Castle (SY669885)

Probably the most significant site in the whole of the South Dorset Ridgeway area – and the most famous. it has long been recognised as one of the largest Iron Age hillforts in Europe, with an internal area the size of 50 football pitches.

The hill on which the Iron Age people settled in around 600 BC, had long been of importance to their ancestors. Sir Mortimer Wheeler, who famously excavated the site between 1934 and 1937, was surprised to discover remains from an earlier time below

Maiden Castle from the east.

the Iron Age remains. The site was excavated again in 1985-6 by Niall Sharples for English Heritage, who are now the guardians of the hillfort.

In the Early Neolithic (4000 BC) the hill was cleared of woodland cover and a causewayed enclosure was constructed (see page 17). This 'oval' earthwork would have required a well-developed system of social organisation and time to construct. It could have been used as a meeting place or have had ritual significance, used for flint tool making or perhaps even for the practice of the laying out of the dead. There are long barrows (burial mounds) nearby and there may have been another one within the enclosure where two infant burials were later discovered.

Some time after the enclosure had stopped being used a bank barrow was built, part of which lies over the enclosure's western end. This bank barrow is one of three on the Ridgeway; the others marking the Ridgeway's ends at Martin's Down and Broadmayne. At 546 metres it is the longest and may mark the territory of a central group or community in the area. The barrow would have been a prominent feature in the landscape for the next two thousand years or so. In the Bronze Age the site retained some ceremonial significance with the placing of round barrows on and around the hill.

The Iron Age hillfort was built around and on top of these earlier monuments, and construction took place over three phases. The earliest part, built around 600 BC was placed over the remains of the causewayed enclosure at the eastern end of the hill. At this time there was just a single rampart surrounding the community that lived within it. The fort was then extended to the western end, doubling in size. It was densely populated; archaeologists have shown that the round houses were laid out in a regular pattern with streets in between. Later the ramparts were rebuilt on a much larger scale and the entrances became more complex (see page 21).

In the later Iron Age the power and influence of Maiden Castle seems to have faded, the community shrunk in size and the occupation of the site moved back into the eastern part of the hill. The settlement extended into the front of the eastern gateway area and it is here that people were living at the time of the Roman Conquest in AD 43. Over 50 human burials have also been found on the site, many within a cemetery at the eastern end. One of the most remarkable finds was an adult male with a Roman ballista bolt lodged in his spine. The remains are now on display at Dorset County Museum.

Occupation of Maiden Castle declined after the Roman Conquest. By the time the army had moved on from Dorchester in about AD 75 the hillfort was abandoned and the Roman town of Durnovaria had been established. The hill was still used for grazing, as it is today.

Maiden Castle is under the care of English Heritage and has open access.

Maumbury Rings (SY690899)

Dorchester's Roman amphitheatre was identified as a Late Neolithic henge during excavations between 1908 and 1913. The town is very visible from both the South Dorset Ridgeway and Maiden Castle and the land between the ridge and the River Frome would have been the home of small farmsteads and settlements throughout the pre-Roman period. The construction of this monument and two others nearby is extremely intriguing; however the importance of this Neolithic ceremonial centre is only recently beginning to be understood.

Henges were monuments built towards the latter part of the Neolithic from about 2500 BC. They take the form of a circular earthwork with a bank and internal ditch with one or more entrances and their scale suggests a much organised society. They are similar

John Hodgson's illustration of the first phase of development at Maumbury Rings, 2500 to 2000 BC.

Poundbury Camp (SY682911)

This Iron Age hillfort sits in a commanding position overlooking the River Frome to the west of Dorchester. There were double banks and ditches on three sides enclosing an area of about 6 hectares but this has been reduced to a single steep-side bank visible today. The ramparts were revetted in timber with later stone walling. There appears to have been one original entrance on the eastern side. An outer rampart may have been levelled during the construction of an aqueduct by the Roman army in the first century AD to bring water from Frampton to Dorchester. The line of the aqueduct is still visible on the hillside.

Poundbury Camp is easily accessible from Poundbury Road leading west from Dorchester town centre. It is an open access area.

enough to causewayed enclosures to suggest they took over from both Maiden Castle and another site in Dorchester at Flagstones (SY704899) as the ritual and meeting centres for this area, although it is unlikely that all three were used at the same time.

The henge at Maumbury Rings had just one entrance to the north-east, with an external bank and ditch. The monument was heavily adapted by the Roman army for use as an amphitheatre, holding as many as 5000 people, and was again modified during the 1640s when it was used as an artillery fort by the Parliamentarian army during the English Civil War. It is now used for community events such as the 2010 Dorchester Roman Festival.

Maumbury Rings is easily accessible to the south of Dorchester Town Centre.

Bincombe Bumps (SY689846)

The antiquarian writer John Hutchins noted in 1774;

'On the downs to the north-east of this place are a great number of barrows of different dimensions, some in groups and some single. From the summit of the Bincombe barrows there is one of the most extensive and beautiful views in the country' The History & Antiquities of the County of Dorset

He must be referring to Bincombe Bumps (SY689846), a group of round barrows that lie on the prominent ridge of Bincombe Hill. The barrows here are reputed to be musical, if you place your ear to the top of the largest at midday, you will hear music.

The South Dorset Ridgeway National Trail passes across the top of Bincombe Down and into the village of Bincombe itself. Bincombe Bumps are in an area of open access land accessible from the trail.

Chalbury Hillfort (SY694838)

This small Iron Age hillfort is recorded as being one of the oldest in the country, with the earliest evidence of occupation in the late Bronze Age and with possible later Romano-British inhabitants.

Constructed in about 600 BC it had a single rampart and one original entrance in the south-east. Two Bronze Age round barrows survived the construction and seem to have been respected through the extensive occupation of the hillfort. The site was abandoned between 400 and 300 BC, just as Maiden Castle was expanding. Perhaps the community moved north over the ridge into the large settlement there.

On the same spur of land known as Rimbury Ridge lies a Bronze Age cremation cemetery discovered by workmen in the nineteenth century. Subsequent excavation found a total of 100 pottery urns associated with burials that were similar in style to those found at Deverel Barrow in Milborne St Andrew.

Chalbury Hillfort is set within an area of open access land on Coombe Valley Road. The South Dorset Ridgeway National Trail and footpaths from Sutton Poyntz pass through.

The barrow group known locally as Bincombe bumps are clearly visible in the centre of the photograph.

Despite its unassuming appearance in this photograph this is the small but nevertheless interesting Chalbury Hillfort, viewed from Coombe Valley Road.

Culliford Tree (SY699855)

This is perhaps one of the most well-known Bronze Age round barrows along the South Dorset Ridgeway. A large bowl barrow, it later gave its name to the Saxon hundred, and became the meeting point or moot for an administrative area that included Clandon, West Knighton, Fryermayne, Little Mayne, Osmington and the now deserted Winterborne villages. In 1740 the barrow was planted with a tree ring. It was excavated in 1858 by Captain Damer and

LEFT Culliford Tree barrow is also recorded as a musical barrow, where 'the sweetest melody' can be heard at midday.

BELOW LEFT Broadmayne Bank barrow is surrounded by several later Bronze Age round barrows. The bank barrow appears to be truncated by the road, but there is no evidence that it continued any further. Culliford Tree is at the top of the photograph below the woodland.

the Reverend William Barnes of Winterborne Came (better known as the Dorset dialect poet). They recorded their excavation and discovered four skeletons. One, a female had an amber and gold necklace, possibly Anglo-Saxon in origin. Several feet below these burials they discovered an early Bronze Age collared urn, containing ashes and human remains. Re-use of barrows by later residents is not unknown; both Saxon and Roman burials have been discovered in the barrows across the Ridgeway.

The barrow is part of a larger group of round barrows placed next to two earlier Neolithic sites, a long barrow (SY699856) to the north which also has a bowl barrow placed on top, and the Broadmayne Bank Barrow to the east.

Culliford Tree barrow group is situated on private land which is crossed by a footpath from a minor road (SY699854) to Came Wood.

Broadmayne Bank Barrow (SY703853)
This bank barrow marks the eastern end of the Ridgeway, mirroring the barrow at Martin's Down in the west. It has been suggested that it was a territorial marker for those living in the area. The barrow was constructed in the Neolithic, perhaps on the site of an earlier long barrow. There are at least two other long barrows close by at Culliford Tree (SY699856) and above Bincombe Hill (SY688851). The bank

barrow is 180 metres long and about 16 metres wide. Although on private land it can easily be seen from Chalky Road (SY701852)

Osmington White Horse (SY715843)

The Osmington White Horse was carved into the chalk of the South Dorset Ridgeway in 1808. In a prominent position above Weymouth Bay it commemorates the visits of George III to the town. The image of the king on his favourite grey charger has long been the subject of local myth and legend; many commentators have argued over dates and details of the construction. Was it the work of one man who later committed suicide from the shame of depicting the much loved monarch leaving the town rather than arriving? Was it cut by soldiers camped on the hill during the Napoleonic wars in 1815? Is it in fact a more ancient chalk figure carved before the Romans came? These stories may well be more romantic than the truth – but well-documented newspaper reports and even a visitor's journal can confirm that the landowner John Wood commissioned local architect James Hamilton to carry out the work. Hamilton also designed the King's Statue in Weymouth. The horse was cut between May and August 1808 by a team of workers directed by Hamilton and paid for by a man called John Ranier.

The surrounding area is also recognised as a Site of Special Scientific Interest for the herb-rich grassland which supports a wide number of rare butterflies, especially the Adonis blue and the Lulworth skipper.

The Osmington White Horse lies on a hill below the South Dorset Ridgeway National Trail and can be reached by footpaths that go to the side and below. The hill figure is also visible from Weymouth seafront.

Paragliders over the Osmington White Horse.

WALKING THE RIDGEWAY

The South Dorset Ridgeway is part of the South West Coast Path National Trail and was the original route to be designated; the route around Portland was only added in 2003. The path offers 630 miles of coastal walking from Minehead to the shores of Poole Harbour. The

The beach at West Bexington, where the South Dorset Ridgeway National Trail meets the sea.

Ridgeway is included as part of the National Trail because it provides stunning views of the Jurassic Coast and the opportunity to explore one of the UK's most significant ancient ceremonial landscapes.

It is possible to walk the whole length (17 miles/ 27 km) from West Bexington to Osmington Mills, or vice-versa, in one day. However it is easy to plan a shorter route, for an afternoon or morning's walk or cycle. There are numerous footpaths and bridleways that cross the Ridgeway, alongside other longer, named routes such as the Macmillan or Jubilee Trails that pass by historic landmarks. The whole of the South Dorset Ridgeway is included on the Ordnance Survey Explorer Map OL15.

For circular walks and suggestions for other routes visit www.southdorsetridgeway.org.uk.

Parking is limited along the Ridgeway, with public car parking at West Bexington Beach and a private car park at The Smugglers Inn at Osmington Mills. It is possible to park in some villages, however the area is well served by bus services from Weymouth and Dorchester to Bridport (First Bus routes X53 and 31). The frequent services mean it is easy to plan a circular walk from one of the villages or a linear route between them. If you use public transport always plan your route with the timetable in mind. Bus and train information is available from Traveline, Tel: 0871 200 2233 www.travelinesw.com. The nearest train stations are in Dorchester and Weymouth.

When walking please wear suitable footwear, take refreshments and waterproofs with you. Remember that in wet weather some of the Ridgeway paths can become very muddy. Refreshments are available at cafés or village and farm shops in Abbotsbury, Martinstown, Upwey and Broadmayne. There are also public houses in Portesham, Martinstown and Sutton Poyntz and a seasonal catering concession at Black Down.

ACKNOWLEDGEMENTS

We would like to thank the authors of the excellent short essays, the Dorset AONB Team, Claire Pinder and Colin Blythe for help with the text, and the staff at Dorchester Library and the Dorset History Centre who helped with finding sources.

Many thanks also to the following for allowing the use of illustrations: David Bailey: pages 9, 11, 14, 28, 29 (both), 30 (bottom), 32, 34 (both), 35, 36 (top), 50, 53, 69, 70; Lisa Berkshire: page 13; Iain Cameron: pages 2/3; Dorset Area of Outstanding Natural Beauty Partnership: pages 15 (top left), 19, 20, 23, 38, 42, 55, 57, 61, 67 (bottom), 68 (top); Dorset County Council: page 24 (bottom); Dorset County Museum: pages 22, 48; Dorset Geological Association: page 15; Dovecote Press Collection: pages 30 (top), 31, 37, 40 (left), 60 (inset), 62; Peter Emery: page 16; English Heritage: pages 17 (N061013), 18 (NMR 18766/11, SY7189/19), 21 (N061014), 26 (NMR 23707/10, SY5987/45), 27 (NMR 23819/17, SY5788/13), 36 (right) (NMR 24500/22, SY6289/3), 54 (NMR 18882/29, SY5 791/40), 64 (NMR 23025, SY6788/138), 67 (NMR 24498/31, SY884/9), 68 (bottom) (NMR SY7095/32/1); Tony Fincham: page 49; Steve Fooks: page 60; Mike Franklin: page 63; John Hodgson: pages 18 (right), 66; Yvonne Lee: pages 8, 20 (left); Peter Lightfoot: maps pages 4, 52; Sue Macpherson, ARPS: pages 1, 6, 7, 10, 39, 40, 41 (right), 54 (bottom), 56 (left), 58; Peter Moore: pages 17 (bottom), 44 (all), 45 (all), 46 (all); Tom Munro: page 43; Oxford Archaeology: page 25; Dave Penman: pages 24, 59; Francesca Radcliffe/Dorset County Museum: page 56 (right) (FR76.08); John Walker: page 51; Wessex Archaeology: page 17 (top left); Ian West: page 15 (top right).

THE SOUTH DORSET RIDGEWAY HERITAGE PROJECT

The significance of the South Dorset Ridgeway was celebrated with a successful Heritage Project from 2008 to 2011 run by the Dorset Area of Outstanding Natural Beauty Partnership. The project supported archaeological and local history research, developed walks and audio trails, events and workshops and resources for schools. Funding was provided by the Heritage Lottery Fund, Natural England and Bournemouth University.

The Dorset Area of Outstanding Natural Beauty is a collection of some of the most varied and distinctive landscapes in the country shaped over time by nature and people. The AONB covers 42% of the county, stretching from Lyme Regis to Poole Harbour and up to Blandford Forum to the north. As well as being a place of great views and beautiful countryside, it's a home for almost 70,000 people and a great source of the essentials – food, water and energy – too. The Dorset AONB Partnership brings together a range of organisations to care for the area and keep it good shape for future generations. The Dorset AONB is one of a family of 47 protected landscapes in England and Wales, set up to conserve and enhance the natural beauty of the landscape.

For more information about the South Dorset Ridgeway and the work of the Dorset Area of Outstanding Natural Beauty visit www.dorsetaonb.org.uk

Sarah Harbige is currently the South Dorset Ridgeway Heritage Project Officer with the Dorset AONB team. Sarah has over 15 years experience of working in museums and heritage and has also worked in education and training. She has published several museum guides and historic photograph books, and grew up in sight of the South Dorset Ridgeway.

Tom Munro manages the Dorset Area of Outstanding Natural Beauty team, with whom he's worked since 2005. With a background in agriculture, woodland management and sustainable land management, he is an outdoor enthusiast, often to be found on the South Dorset Ridgeway either on bike or on foot.

First published in 2011 by The Dovecote Press Ltd
Stanbridge, Wimborne Minster, Dorset BH21 4JD

ISBN 978-1-904-34991-4

Typeset in FS Ingrid designed by The Dovecote Press Ltd
Printed and bound by GraphyCems, Navarra

All papers used by The Dovecote Press are natural, recyclable products made from wood grown in sustainable, well-managed forests

A CIP catalogue record for this book is available from the British Library

1 3 5 7 9 8 6 4 2

COVER ILLUSTRATIONS
FRONT
Chalbury, Green Hill, Bincombe and Weymouth Bay from the flank of the South Dorset Ridgeway (David Bailey).
BACK
Maiden Castle in the Iron Age (English Heritage (N061014);
Adonis blue butterfly (Peter Moore); Hardy Monument (Steve Fooks);
Osmington White Horse (David Bailey).